THE CHILDREN OF
BUCHENWALD

THE CHILDREN OF BUCHENWALD

CHILD SURVIVORS OF THE HOLOCAUST

AND THEIR POST-WAR LIVES

BY

JUDITH HEMMENDINGER

AND

ROBERT KRELL

gefen גפן
publishing house בית הוצאה לאור
JERUSALEM ◆ NEW YORK

Copyright © Gefen Publishing House
Jerusalem 2000/5760

Typesetting: Marzel A.S. – Jerusalem
Cover Design: Studio Paz, Jerusalem

1 3 5 7 9 8 6 4 2

Gefen Publishing House
POB 36004, Jerusalem 91360, Israel
972-2-538-0247 • isragefe@netvision.net.il

Gefen Books
12 New Street Hewlett, NY 11557, USA
516-295-2805 • gefenbooks@compuserve.com

www.israelbooks.com

Printed in Israel

Send for our free catalogue

ISBN 965-229-246-X

Library of Congress Cataloging-in-Publication Data:
Krell Robert, Hemmendinger Judith
The children of Buchenwald : child survivors and their postwar lives/
Judith Hemmendinger, Robert Krell
1. Holocaust survivors – New York (State) – Biography. 2. Holocaust survivors – France –
Biography. 3. Holocaust survivors – Israel – Biography. 4. Refugees, Jewish – Biography.
5. Holocaust, Jewish (1939-1945) – Influence. 6. Jewish children in the Holocaust.
7. Buchenwald (Concentration camp) I. Krell, Robert II Title.
F130.J5H46 2000 • 940.53'18'092243224 – dc21 • [B] 00-027674 CIP

CONTENTS

Acknowledgements

*T*he authors are fortunate to have supportive families and friends who demonstrate patience with our preoccupations. We thank them for their understanding. We are grateful for financial support in publishing this new edition of a remarkable story. One source was the Leo Krell Memorial Book Fund of the Vancouver Holocaust Education Centre, the other, George Goldbloom of Miami, one of the Buchenwald children, whose generosity helped us achieve our objective.

We are indebted also to Francesca Wilson for typing all drafts of the manuscript, to Leanne Nash for her critical reading of it, to David Reed for selected translations from the French, and to Jerry Kapelus (of Toronto) another Buchenwald child, who provided photos and insights.

A special thanks to Robbie Waisman, who read the draft, commented and offered us his photo album — the source of many images in this book. Robbie is also a Buchenwald survivor.

Anonymity was respected with all accounts derived from the original 1981 doctoral thesis where each child or adolescent is given a first name, not necessarily his own. The detailed life stories of Romek and Lulek are offered with their permission. Over time, names have changed somewhat to adapt to the countries of settlement and common usage. So to George Goldbloom (Idel Goldblum), Jerry Kapelus (Jakob Kapelusz) and Robbie Waisman (Romek Wajsman) and all the boys, our gratitude — you are an inspiration to us all.

We thank everyone represented in these pages for their accounts, knowing how painful it was to recapture memories of terrible times. Some accounts were obtained twenty, forty, even fifty years after liberation, and their lives continue to unfold. We appreciate their courage and dignity.

Judith Hemmendinger
Robert Krell

A Reflection

by Robert Krell

*A*s a child survivor of the Holocaust (in hiding in Holland) and as a child psychiatrist, I was readily captivated by this extraordinary story. Of 1,000 children discovered at Buchenwald on April 11, 1945, 426 were sent on a transport to France about two months later. For the most part, they were viewed as damaged beyond hope of repair, of recovery, of normalcy.

At that time physicians, psychologists and social workers encountered children who were living skeletons, the remnants of hundreds of thousands of Jewish children brutalized beyond belief or comprehension and murdered. They could barely be distinguished from the dead, certainly not from each other, with shaven heads, blank stares and emaciated bodies.

Some mental health workers considered them psychopaths, assuming they must have been selfish or manipulative or mean-spirited in order to survive when so many others died.

Assumptions were made, allegations whispered, theories expounded and few were challenged.

Yet, somehow, over time, this group of orphans, bereft of family and home, of security and nourishment, of identity and self-worth, defied the dire predictions forecast for them. These 426 children and adolescents have produced rabbis and scholars, physicists and physicians, businessmen and artists, as well as a Nobel Prize winner. The majority have become devoted husbands and fathers. Of course there were some who did not recover, did not succeed. And some were hospitalized, others committed suicide. That was to be expected given their gruesome experiences and never-ending nightmares. What was not expected is that so many, despite suffering depressions and insomnia, fears and anxiety, would show such resilience and determination. It is a story that must be known and repeated.

In 1981, at the World Gathering of Jewish Holocaust Survivors in Jerusalem, I heard Rabbi Lau describe himself as one of the youngest survivors of Buchenwald — age eight years old at liberation. It was my privilege to meet the rabbi in 1994 and to re-introduce him to my friend, Robbie Waisman who was 14 in the Spring of 1945. So it was that Lulek met Romek. Their accounts are in this book and they are in the group photo of young child survivors on the cover.

I read Judith Hemmendinger's book translated into Dutch in 1984 and English in 1985. When I called this gracious lady suggesting we re-issue this compelling work with additional accounts and photos, she agreed enthusiastically. Since that call we have worked together to bring to the reader this new edition.

As a child psychiatrist who has seen many children ravaged in their developmental years, some in childhood, others in adolescence, I am overwhelmed by the accomplishments of the Buchenwald children. How did they do it? What and who helped? I know of their struggle with silence. How did they learn to talk again? I know of their mistrust and suspiciousness of people. How did they learn to trust again? I know of their grief, their bereavement. How did they learn to love again? I know of their rage. How did they regain compassion? How did they learn to play again and pray again?

Where did they find the courage? Did it come from memories of a loving home, a family Shabbat, familiarity with traditions? How did they recapture the before and link it to the after. How did they cross the abyss and make it to the other side?

If these "doomed" souls contributed so much, what might have been the contribution of the one and one-half million children who were robbed of their chance to live and dream?

I'm not convinced any of us will truly understand the depths of their despair in the tragedy which enfolded them nor the height of their triumphs achieved against such overwhelming odds. Surely it should inspire examination of one's own life and encourage one to live it meaningfully. Their struggle deserves a meaningful response.

FOREWORD

BY ELIE WIESEL

Dear Judith,

I read your book, and I remember. I see us back in 1945. Écouis, Ambloy, Taverny. The dumbfounded instructors, the disoriented children. Did you know that to us, you belonged to another universe? Everything separated us: the language, the physical circumstances, and above all, the memories.

Did you know Judith, that we pitied you? We felt sorry for you. I hope you are not angry that I speak so openly? You thought you could educate us, and yet the younger of us knew more than the oldest amongst you, about what existed in the world, of the futility of life, the brutal triumph of death. We were not impressed with your age, or your authority. We observed you with amusement and mistrust. We felt ourselves stronger than you.

How did you succeed, Judith, to tame us? How did Niny, the beautiful, young, dedicated teacher, put up with us? I think often about what we went through together and then I feel embarrassed. It must have been so difficult for you to find for all of us a path, and a possibility for understanding each other.

I often dream of the months, the years I spent in the children's homes of the OSE.[1] The first Shabbat meals, the walks, the campfires, the songs, the gatherings. I will never forget the festival days at Ambloy, reciting Kaddish together, the fast of Yom Kippur, the joy of Simchat Torah, a forced joy at first but later genuine.

You recall it all so well, Judith. The departure of the children, the trains, the dreams, the nightmares. It was a remarkable community, in constant ferment. We were all possessed with the same longing, namely to succeed. Moishe-Ber,

---

1. OSE = Oeuvre de Secours aux Enfants. The OSE was a Society devoted to providing help to children.

Menashe, Kalman, Binem and the children of Glick. Someday I shall also try to relate, in my own way, the stories that link us to yours.

Do you still remember Shushani? The lessons of the Talmud, the heated debates? Should we adapt to modern life or not? Should we go to the Holy Land or to an uncle in Brooklyn? I still recall my first report, "The Ghetto — Danger or Temptation," which I delivered in Yiddish. André Bodner advised me: "The structure, keep in mind the structure."

The choral group, I also remember the choir very well. Shy as I was, I had to feign anger in order to maintain control. Every recital caused me sleepless nights. I lacked confidence and authority. I could not turn away any boy or girl even if they sang badly. Moreover, I could not look a choir girl in the eye; they all looked so pretty and inaccessible. I realised I must have appeared stupid indeed.

Now I understand that you also, the leaders, had obstacles to surmount and problems to solve. It could not have been easy to educate a group of children like us, with our peculiarities and obsessions. Nor did you have guidelines.

In reality it came down to a challenge of you against us. It was understandable that it might fail. How would we find common ground? Emerging from darkness we could not rid ourselves of it. Nor did we want to. Uprooted, underprivileged, we longed to remain faithful to the dead. In that time, the survivors had nothing to say to the living. The victory over the Germany of Hitler and his accomplices was celebrated in Europe and the rest of the world, without us.

Locked into the solitude of a mutilated, violated childhood, we longed to be let alone. When a representative of the outside world attempted to reach us, we withdrew further. We refused to cooperate with you.

We did not want your help, your understanding, your psychosocial investigations, or your charity. You entered our lives too soon; we were still in mourning.

Reasonably, Judith, we were doomed to live cloistered lives on the other side of the wall. And yet we succeeded in a short time to find ourselves on the same side. To whom can we attribute the miracle? How can one explain it? To our belief? To yours?

The fact is that all the children could have chosen violence or nihilism but you succeeded to direct us toward confidence and reconciliation. You supported and encouraged us to choose a stake in the future and community. Your book demonstrates this. Their successes have justified your gamble. You bet on us to recover. I love how you talk of their family life, the wife of one, the children of another.

I have kept in touch with a few. We often recall our time in Ambloy and Taverny. We speak of you, of Niny and of other leaders. In my travels, when I meet someone from the homes, I take them aside and talk.

I am happy that you wrote this book, Judith. It is serious and disconcerting. Occasionally it also made me laugh.

Judith, do you realise how much you meant to our existence?

Elie Wiesel (1984)

INTRODUCTION

by Judith Hemmendinger

*O*ne summer day in 1945, a photograph taken in the port of Haifa was published in Haaretz, an Israeli newspaper. It showed a little eight-year old boy, standing by a small suitcase, holding a toy gun. He was one of the children who had been found at Buchenwald by American soldiers. Lulek was waiting for his older brother, Naphtali, who had left momentarily to fetch the rest of their luggage from customs.

Lulek was going to shoot, with his toy gun, anyone who tried to take his bag. When a man carrying a camera (an object he had never seen before) approached him, he starting shooting at him, convinced the man was going to steal his belongings.

An eight-year-old survivor of Buchenwald? Yes. One and a half million babies and children died of starvation in the ghettos and were murdered in the concentration camps and by Einsatzgruppen and Nazi collaborators throughout Europe. Of the several thousand children to survive concentration camps, Lulek was one.

I was head of one of the homes rented by the OSE and assisted in their return to normal life. The past experiences of these children created an extremely delicate situation with which we had to deal. Many of my charges later in life recalled their time with us as a period of transition spanning a bridge between the camps and a new life.

It was a period of only two years, intense and meaningful years.

By the end of 1947, the Castle of Vaucelles in Taverny was closed. Its occupants left to build a new life, in unfamiliar countries, often bereft of family or support. Where did these children and teenagers find the strength to cope with an unfamiliar society, a new language, and a new environment? How did they find a career, a means to earn a living, start a family, and raise children? How did they "manage, despite a destructive beginning, despite the losses and

Judith Hemmendinger, Director of Home at Amboly and at Taverny

the grief, to achieve success in the quest of normality and to survive after survival?"[1]

When I came to settle in Jerusalem, Israel in 1970, I was frequently invited, as a social worker, to conferences of psychiatrists and psychologists. There was always a lecture about the "poor" survivors who were discussed primarily in terms of psychopathology — even labelled "psychopathic!"

Despite my imperfect Hebrew, I would point out that not all survivors were psychopaths or suffered total psychological impairment. I was challenged to show that there were "normal" citizens. The professionals claimed not to have met any, only sick ones and that others simply refused to speak about their experiences, employing the defence-mechanism of denial. I knew that "my" children would talk because they trusted me. Information was needed to demonstrate that not all survivors were hopeless and helpless, a group of people to be written off.

I turned to Elie Wiesel for advice and he suggested I interview children from the hostel and write a doctoral dissertation based on the findings.[2] I created a questionnaire with over 100 questions related to pre-war, war and post-war experiences and began to "interview" my former children, in the United States, France and Israel. Not all agreed to participate, but approximately 60 responded, saying, "How can we say no to you?" However, they would not answer the questionnaire, insisting on offering their accounts free from restrictions. They could not conceive of trying to summarise their lives in a few lines, reducing their unimaginable experiences to brief answers in response to clinical questions.

It left me only one two-part question: What happened to you from the day you were liberated and from the day you left the hostel? I tape recorded and wrote down each account and contacted my professor in Strasbourg, the supervisor for my doctoral dissertation. It was accepted practice to base a dissertation on statistics. However, when I explained that I had 60 interviews, each account representing a deeply personal life experience, exclusive to that

---

1. Robert Krell. Psychological reverberations of the Holocaust in the lives of child survivors. The 1997 Monna and Otto Weinman lecture. Published by the United States Holocaust Memorial Museum Research Institute, Washington.
2. Judith Hemmendinger. Rehabilitation of young camp survivors after the death camps. Strasbourg, France: University of Strasbourg, 1981.

person and impossible to reduce to statistics, he allowed me to present 15 accounts, five each of boys now established in the United States, Paris and Israel.

In 1981, I presented my thesis at the Faculty of Human Sciences of the University of Strasbourg and received my doctorate Cum Laude. The local papers reported on an unusual and interesting dissertation called "After the Death Camps, Re-entry Into Life."

Two years later, in Jerusalem, I was visited by the Swiss Director of "Terre des Hommes" — an international children's help organisation. He began to read the dissertation, asked to take it back to Lausanne and called to say he had an editor to publish "these interesting accounts." And so it happened that in 1984 a book was published in Lausanne by Éditions Favre, titled "Les Enfants de Buchenwald," despite my warnings to Mr. Favre that people were no longer interested in Holocaust memoirs and he would likely lose money. He insisted, offering three compelling reasons. Being very young, for him the war seemed long ago and he was surprised to know there were some camp survivors still alive. As a Catholic, he knew few Jews and had developed an interest to know more about what had happened and, as a Swiss citizen, he wanted to know what took place in Nazi-occupied countries around "neutral" Switzerland. He was sure that the stories were of interest, that I should write in a "living style" and remember that the first sentence is the most important. He assured me it would be a best-seller and I should have it translated into other languages. And it did sell very well. However, in order to stay within the allowed 200 pages, I could only offer the bare facts of the fascinating life stories.

Dr. Robert Krell first read the book in the Dutch version, "De Kinderen van Buchenwald." Since it is no longer available in any language, he proposed to re-issue the book, including as co-author a broader perspective on child survivors generally and several updated accounts with commentary and pictures.

Today, many of the children of Buchenwald are grandfathers. It is still difficult for them to offer their life stories — even to their families. So they send me their grandchildren, to learn more about them from me. To them, Dr. Krell and I dedicate this book.

We wish for them to take pride in their grandfathers, from whose courage and resilience they, and all of us, can learn a great deal.

A Biography of
Judith Hemmendinger

by Robert Krell

*E*lie Wiesel, in his foreword, poses the question: "How did you succeed, Judith, to tame us?"

What indeed are the qualities one must possess to face children and adolescents returned from a world which defies the imagination of those who were not there?

And yet, could one who *was* there, provide the humane ingredients necessary to help recapture trust, self-esteem, ordinary joy and a renewed respect for life — and for death. I think not. It was Judith and *her* qualities that were needed, and those of her closest colleague, Niny Wolf.

Judith Hemmendinger was born Judith Feist on October 2, 1923, in Bad-Homburg, a resort area near Frankfurt, Germany. Her parents were Orthodox Jews. Her father was a mining engineer and her mother held a doctorate in Zoology and Botany from Heidelberg. Judith was the second of five children born between 1922-1928. They lived in a big villa surrounded by a huge garden in which the children played all day. She recalls her childhood as "golden."

When she was six years old, the entire family moved to Paris because her father was offered a good job. Her life changed dramatically. She felt her childhood was over. She had to contend with a new language, neighbours and other children. Judith's life was divided in two. At home the family was Jewish and spoke German. At school she had a secular education and spoke French. In retrospect, she now realises that this dual world actually enriched her life and increased her tolerance for other people. In 1933, when Hitler rose to power in Germany, fleeing Jews arrived as refugees to their home in Paris. They related sad stories about the Reich's pogroms and the horrors of the first camps:

Dachau and Buchenwald where they had been imprisoned until their immigration.

From that time, Judith has suffered from insomnia.

When war broke out in September 1939, her father was immediately arrested by the French authorities and imprisoned as an enemy because he was still a German citizen (it was very difficult to obtain French citizenship). When the Germans occupied France, Judith's father was imprisoned in another camp as a Jew, and eventually deported to Auschwitz in September 1943 where he was murdered. The family had lost their home, were without money and relied on selling their remaining belongings. They went into hiding, the two youngest children with their mother and the three older children each in a separate place.

Judith worked in an OSE hostel for hidden children. She was 18 years old. Then she was hidden in an agricultural school organised by Jews as a hiding place. There she met Claude, her future husband.

After Judith's father was deported, her mother insisted on crossing the Swiss border with her two younger children and she asked Judith to accompany her because she was afraid to go alone. It was a dangerous journey but they succeeded in entering Switzerland through the Alps. There Judith was in a refugee camp until the OSE helped her obtain a six-month course in social work in Geneva, which prepared workers for after the war.

In Geneva her work consisted of welcoming the small children who arrived illegally into Switzerland and finding out their real names so that they could be returned to parents or family after the war.

In May 1945, OSE Geneva received a cable from Chaplain Marcus of the American Army stating that he found in Buchenwald a barracks with 1,000 Jewish children. He asked the OSE to bring them quickly out of the Camp.

As a refugee, Judith had to leave Switzerland. Back in France she decided to visit the Buchenwald boys whose names she had seen on the long lists sent to Geneva. She arrived on a Thursday in one of their hostels that sheltered about 90 boys and she stayed for Shabbat. They no longer had a home. Neither did she. So Judith decided to build together with them "our home." The OSE soon asked her to be the Director and she stayed until September 1947 when the last boy left.

In the meantime, her mother had returned to France and waited for her husband's return. She jumped at the ring of the doorbell or phone, certain he had come back. In 1949 she lost hope that he had survived and joined her two sons in their kibbutz in Israel. There she returned to her love of botany learned in Heidelberg and planted trees and flowers. Her kibbutz is exceptionally green and she lies buried on a hill in a graveyard she herself had prepared.

Judith did not know where to go when Taverny closed. She was 24. She went to England to visit her uncle (her father's brother had left Germany in 1933) and she worked at his office until she married Claude Hemmendinger in September 1948.

Claude had escaped from France to Spain, crossing the Pyrenees in 1944. From there he went to Palestine and joined the Jewish army. He was injured during a riot in 1947, spent many months in hospital and was sent back to his parents in Strasbourg to recover. That is where Judith and Claude met again and married.

They returned to Israel, to his kibbutz near Beit She'an, near the Jordan. Their daughter Lea was born there. They were very happy. When Claude's father died, they returned to Strasbourg to look after his mother and to settle the business. A temporary stay turned into 20 years. Two sons were born and for ten years Judith stayed at home. She returned to work as a personnel officer. Her insomnia continued to trouble her and Judith entered psychotherapy with a psychoanalyst which helped her to speak about the past and enabled her to write about the children of Buchenwald.

Eventually, the Hemmendinger family returned to Israel in September 1969. Judith began formal studies, achieving her B.A. at Jerusalem, her M.A. from Bar-Ilan and her Ph.D. in 1981 from Strasbourg.

Their three children live in Jerusalem. They have seventeen grandchildren, two of whom are already married.

Judith is also a licensed tour guide and twice a year, on Succot and Passover, she hires a bus for the entire family to tour together for a day. That way all the cousins get to know each other.

She remains at work, looking after the welfare of the elderly. She is happy to be with her husband, with her own family, and with the families of the Buchenwald children, and to have at last a permanent home.

It takes a special person to respond at a time of need. Judith's personal life experiences, her hiding in France, escape to Switzerland, refugee status, work with little children all alone in the world, provided her with the necessary sensitivity and good sense combined with her caring nature to win over the boys from Buchenwald and return to them a sense of dignity and self-worth. Throughout her life, Judith has maintained and nurtured these qualities into a lifetime of service to those in need, from children to the elderly.

How fortunate are those who have known her.

FROM AUSCHWITZ
TO LIBERATION

O n April 11, 1945, American troops arrived at Buchenwald. War-toughened soldiers, prepared for battle, stood transfixed. They were not prepared for this. Thousands of starving, skeletal men were heaped together in barrack cots, waiting to join the piles of skeletons outside. The soldiers went from barracks to barracks until they reached number 66. What they saw there magnified their horror. Hundreds of children, all boys, silently gazed at them with huge, deep-set eyes from faces resembling those of elderly men. They were Jewish children from Poland and Hungary aged eight to twenty.

The commander of the American troops was totally bewildered and sent a cable to the OSE in Geneva. "Have found a thousand Jewish children in Buchenwald. Take immediate measures to evacuate them." Then I was a refugee working at the OSE in Geneva and made efforts to obtain visas for the children. Switzerland was prepared to take 280 children, France 480, and England 250.[1] The children would be leaving Buchenwald in June.

In the meantime, the Americans provided food and clothing. The youngsters wore the notorious striped pyjamas, often far too large, or the only substitute clothing to be found, uniforms of the Hitler Youth. The kindness of the soldiers had deadly consequences. They stuffed the youngsters with canned foods with high fat content, sweets and chewing gum. The sudden overeating in severely malnourished children resulted in many deaths. Typhus swept through the

---

1. For an excellent description of young concentration camp survivors brought to England, see Martin Gilbert's "The Boys: Triumph Over Adversity," Vancouver/Toronto: Douglas and McIntyre, 1996, and Sarah Moskovitz's "Love Despite Hate: Child Survivors of the Holocaust and Their Adult Lives," New York: Shocken, 1983.

David Perlmutter at age 8 and Stefan-Jerzy Zweig (Juschu) at age 4

camp. The only remedy available was to cover the fever-racked children constantly with fresh sheets.

The experiences of these surviving children were beyond description. Most had been in Auschwitz, treated as severely as adults.[1] They were selected for work if physically strong enough. A typical day consisted of waking between 4.00-5.00 a.m., with thirty minutes to wash (each barracks had only a few faucets) straightening of cots, a watery coffee the only food, and one hour roll-call outside, regardless of weather. Then off to work, marched in rows of five, to rejoin the digging, quarry, and welding groups. Their hard labour was accompanied by the constant beatings from the guards. Newcomers repeatedly tried to escape from their work teams or tried to join others considered less harsh. They were usually caught, cruelly punished or were gassed, if judged unable to work. They soon learned to try to remain unnoticed and meld with the masses.

There was no rest period. When night came, they again formed rows of five to return to camp. Despite total exhaustion, the SS forced them to march by a prisoner orchestra playing merry tunes and waltzes to line up once more for roll call, the terror of every prisoner.

Between 60,000 and 70,000 prisoners stood at attention, hour after hour, in the fierce glare of searchlights, in freezing cold or smouldering heat, while the SS called out their numbers. If a single man was missing, no one could move until he was found. Exhausted prisoners fell to the ground. Their comrades were not allowed to help them. If a prisoner had died at work, the body was dragged back for roll-call. The living and the dead, the SS counted all.

After this nightly ordeal, the prisoners returned to their barracks to receive their daily food ration: a bowl of soup, a little margarine and some bread of which part was saved for the next morning. The starvation diet quickly reduced the prisoners' ability to work. Before long they became "Mussulmen," the living dead, in a state of hopelessness and apathy. The children shied away from them

---

1. For an overview of the war waged against European Jewry, see Martin Gilbert's "The Holocaust: A History of the Jews of Europe During the Second World War," New York: Henry Holt, 1985. Buchenwald is described by Eugen Kogon in "The Theory and Practice of Hell," New York: Berkley Books, 1980.

for fear the condition was infectious and knowing that all such people would soon die in the gas chambers.

The youngest children adapted quickly to life in the camp, realising their chance for survival depended on connections, attachments, on not being alone. Those children, who upon arrival remained with brothers or cousins, tried never to be separated from them, neither in the barracks nor at work. Those without family sought out a companion. Without one, the hard struggle of everyday life was unbearable — mutual moral support being all that was left of connections with being human.

When Auschwitz was evacuated in January 1945, due to the approaching Soviet Army, 61,000 prisoners still able to walk were forced westward. For weeks, they walked on foot through cold and snow, clad in rags and without food. Occasionally they were allowed a few hours of sleep but most of the time they continued, as if sleepwalking. Those who could not continue were shot. The children recall this exodus with particular horror. Upon their arrival in France, they would speak of it only as the "evacuation" for its experience defied description and exceeded even the particular atrocities of Auschwitz and Buchenwald.

In early March 1945, 10,000-12,000 of those who survived the march arrived in Buchenwald, near Weimar, Germany, where the nightmare continued. Food rations were even smaller than in Auschwitz. There were 47,000 inmates in Buchenwald and as the American troops approached, the Germans murdered many prisoners in a nearby forest and herded 26,000 prisoners, mostly Jews, onto 50 railroad cars headed for Dachau, near Munich. All of those on board the train died of hunger, cold, or asphyxiation.

The children who came later to France were survivors of this entire murderous sequence of events. After liberation and still in Buchenwald, some went to German houses in Weimar to ask for food. One of them requested a violin, another, a camera to take photos of Buchenwald. Some stole chickens or bicycles, considering this not to be theft but a sort of compensation. When they wanted to take their "treasures" to France, they were discouraged to do so with the convoy leader promising they would get these as well in France. All of them obeyed except the one child who liked to play Hungarian melodies and who refused to part with his violin.

After liberation, the children were completely bewildered. Most had no surviving family; others had no idea if anyone was still alive. Their future was a mystery. Communist Russia occupied their home countries, Poland and Hungary and the children distrusted the German communists who were also prisoners in Buchenwald.

Most wanted to go to Palestine, the country of the Jews, but it was still a British mandate that refused admission to the refugees.

Therefore, they accepted the proposition of the OSE to go to Switzerland, France or England, free Western European countries. A French train was sent to pick up the children.

The children leaving Buchenwald

The French train.
Written on the side
KL Buchenwald

The French train.
Where are our parents?

2

ARRIVAL

IN FRANCE

When the special French train arrived in Buchenwald on June 2, 1945, children stormed it for fear that it would leave without them. Dr. Revel, who accompanied the children, described that "dressed in their striped pyjamas or in uniforms of the Hitler Youth (the only clothes available), they looked like young savages." Many had suffered a total loss of identity. They did not remember their names, having been addressed only by their numbers or nicknames.

Each time the train stopped, the boys jumped out to pillage the countryside, but once in France, the vandalism stopped. A new problem presented itself when the French spotted the German uniforms and attacked the train. The child survivors, now perceived as the enemy, were in such great danger that the train had to be diverted to a side track overnight at the Metz railroad station. The words "K.L. (Konzentrationlager — Concentration Camp) Buchenwald-Orphans" were painted on the cars.

It took four days for the convoy[1] to reach Écouis in Normandy because the conductor had been instructed to stop whenever the boys wanted to romp through the countryside.

Écouis was an abandoned sanatorium placed at the disposal of the OSE by the French government. The OSE had prepared 500 beds for little children, unaware that nearly 400 were aged 12 to 21 and only 30 were between 8 and 12 years old. They looked like bandits, suspicious and mute. Their heads were shorn; all dressed the same, with faces still swollen from hunger and not a smile to be seen. Their eyes bespoke sadness and suspicion. They were apathetic

---

1. The convoy lists contain 426 names. The heading is "Enfants Venus D'Allemagne-Convoi du 8 Juin 1945" and is appended at the end of this book.

towards the outside world. They likened the supervisors to guards and were terror stricken at the sight of doctors who reminded them of Mengele, the man who, upon their arrival in Auschwitz, had sent the weak ones to gas chambers, the able-bodied to slave labour.

It was clear that Écouis would not function in the manner of more traditional institutions. The youngsters felt entitled to everything that they had been deprived of for so many years. The food they had received from American soldiers was of better quality than what post-war France could offer during the first year. So they bartered in the neighbouring farms for extra food by trading blankets, sheets, dishes and pots from the home. One of them stole puppies that he sold in Paris.

Écouis was a collection of houses surrounding a common yard where all the youngsters were gathered on various occasions. It was at Écouis they vented their anger, their rage. Their rebelliousness led to factions splitting off into groups, by age, by degree of observance and by nationality. The older boys in their late teens and even early twenties were sent to Paris, to a big home on Rue Rollin and to Fontenay-aux-Roses, another place on the outskirts of Paris. They were about 10-15% of the total group.

Unfortunately, the architecture of Écouis reminded the children of the camps. In addition, the Director spoke only French and German and could communicate, barely, only with the Rumanians who knew a little French. All the other boys would not respond when addressed in German. When pieces of bread were handed out, this too reminded them of the camps and they requested that bread be put on the table so that they could help themselves. At the end of each meal the leftovers disappeared into their rooms since one could never know when the next meal would be served.

For these young people, all adults were potential enemies who were not to be trusted. One day they were served Camembert cheese for dessert. The strong smell convinced them that it was poison. They threw the cheese at the adults who were supervising dinner.

There was a group, perhaps about 25-35%, who wanted to keep kosher.[1] They

---

1. Kosher/Kashrut — observing the traditional preparation of food according to Jewish religious practice.

were mainly of Hungarian origin and they went to Ambloy, a small village where there were large homes.

At first no one had thought of kashrut. The struggle focussed on finding the best possible food to help rebuild the strength of the undernourished children. There were arguments and debates for there were those who spoke against returning to traditional religious life. After what they had seen, they had lost faith.

There was also a rift between the boys of Polish origin who had been embroiled in war since 1939 and those of Hungarian background who were hit with full force in 1944. The Polish-born Jews spoke Yiddish while many of the Hungarians did not. Serious fighting and arguments carried over from the camps, where the last arrivals thought the other inmates to be privileged. The personnel were unable to understand their motives or to conceive what the children had experienced, because they talked about the camps only among themselves. Each group stuck with its own.

The boys were not allowed to leave Écouis by the authorities in charge, but they did not necessarily obey. One day, Victor, aged 15, decided to go to Paris with a friend because he had heard about an underground train. He also wanted to visit a centre for returning refugees, the Hotel Lutetia, in the hope of finding members of his family. But of course he wanted to return to Écouis later. He had no other place to go. After a series of adventures they reached their destination. It was a beautiful building and they were given a room with two large beds and a white telephone. There was a knock. A priest entered the room and spoke to them in Polish and Yiddish. They talked for hours.

The next day the priest put the two adventurers back on the train to Écouis and paid their fare. When they returned, they told eager listeners of the wonders of Paris, its huge hotels and white telephones. Victor also reported that the priests all speak Polish and Yiddish, not knowing they had been received by Abbé Glasberg, a Jew of Polish descent who helped many Jews during the war.

In later years, Victor settled in Paris and became an electronics engineer. According to him, it was the white telephone at the Hotel Lutetia that led him to choose his profession.

Colonel Rozen addresses a gathering of children at Ecouis

Ecouis 1945. Israel Lau, Izio Rosenman, David Perlmutter

The French courses organised by the Director were not very successful. Taking French meant that they would remain in France and that idea did not appeal to them. France was too close to Germany and most wanted to leave for Palestine. The English provided visas for the group at Écouis and promised that more would arrive — a promise never fulfilled.

There were many visitors who came to Écouis to talk with the young survivors of Buchenwald. There were journalists and rabbis and numerous officials who came to meet with these earliest arrivals from Germany. As a matter of fact, visitors <u>did</u> want to hear the experiences but the boys refused to speak of them. The children listened silently to the beautiful and affectionate words, noted that it was well meant, but did not react for they were totally disillusioned about human nature.

One day Chaplain Marcus of the American army came to Écouis. He had met the boys before in Buchenwald. They sat in a circle around him on the lawn. The Chaplain stood in front of them unable to utter a word, overcome by his emotions, tears streamed down his cheeks. It had been a long time since the children had seen an adult cry. Something in them thawed and they too began to cry. One of them described later: "The Chaplain returned to us our souls. He reawakened the feelings we had buried within us." So began also the return of family memories that had been deeply buried in the camps. Most of the children came from large, religious families, who observed the Sabbath and did not eat pork, kept a kosher kitchen and were scrupulous about daily prayers. For those old enough to have memories of the happier times before the camps, their faith gave them the courage to gather the energy to recapture a Jewish identity. They chose as spokesman a Jewish instructor named Leo Margulies, who had been in Buchenwald for six years. Because he had managed to retain Jewish traditions under severe oppression, he was held in high esteem by the children. He was virtually the only adult they trusted. It was Mr. Margulies who requested from the Director the provision of kosher food. The Director did not know what to do under the difficult conditions of 1945, and did not think it possible to provide kosher cooking for 500 persons. Mr. Margulies proposed opening a smaller home for those who wanted to abide by the rules of kashrut and the OSE agreed.

Some had applied for kosher food but were reluctant to leave Écouis and

their friends. At the last minute, when
the trucks were about to leave Écouis,
many decided to join and they took
with them 30 of the youngest children
who were undecided. It was there at
Ambloy, the newly established hostel,
where Judith met her charges.

*Israel Lau (Lulek) leaves
for Palestine in 1945*

*Dancing the Hora before
leaving Ecouis for Palestine*

3

THE CHILDREN
AT AMBLOY

Approximately 100 children and adolescents were transferred to the beautiful castle of Ambloy, near the town of Vendome; it was surrounded by an enormous park with forests and a lake. It was there I met the children of Buchenwald. I had just returned to France where I had been living before the war. My father did not return from Auschwitz and the rest of my family was dispersed. In Geneva, I had heard about the existence of the children of Buchenwald and had decided to visit them. I sat on the lawn with them, watching their expressionless faces and apparently not noticing or ignoring my presence. They spoke in Yiddish about the camps, the evacuation from Auschwitz, the long march to Buchenwald and the last days of Barracks 66.[1] The Director of Ambloy was upset about the boys' aggressiveness towards him. Like other Directors of homes for survivors of Buchenwald (called "B homes"), he believed that they were born psychopaths, cold and indifferent by nature and that this was the reason they were able to survive the camps.

The day after my arrival was a Friday, the beginning of the Sabbath, which was celebrated with a special dinner. With the same stern faces, the boys began to sing religious songs connected to the Sabbath meal. They did this with such fire and intensity that I was deeply moved and realised that these were not faces of indifference, but faces marked by a past of unspeakable suffering. I decided to stay in Ambloy and when the Director left, I took over the home with Niny, a young counsellor from Écouis. During the months in Ambloy and later Taverny, our main objective was to restore the boys' faith in humanity and in themselves.

It was clear that all traditional methods of education were bound to fail. We

---

1. Barracks 66 at Buchenwald housed the children and adolescents. It was a place of such terror and misery that it produced a lifetime of nightmares.

Group photo at Ambloy. September 1945.

had to be practical and adapt to the boys. But what good was it to observe them or to show them affection if we could not talk with them? We only spoke German, the language of their tormentors, and definitely could not use it. So we learned Yiddish by carefully listening to their conversations. Even though we did not learn to speak it well, it was much better received than German. We also needed to remember their names. It was a challenge to get to know 100 boys who on first sight all looked similar. Sitting together on the lawn or during meals we would ask them over and over again "What is your name?" Once we were able to say "Hello, Moshe Cohen" or "How are you, Abraham Weiss?" the boy addressed might still remain silent but would also reveal a shy smile. Their identity had been returned to them and this signalled the beginning of communication.

The fights between Hungarians and Poles persisted at Ambloy. Each morning I would watch the injured line up at the infirmary. I would ask them the reasons for their quarrel and would not provide care until they had first made peace. When we thought about what we had been told of life in the camps, we realised how artificial was the organisation of the home (such as the division of dormitories into age groups). We therefore told them they were free to choose their roommates and they formed groups of various sizes based on their home towns. The larger dormitories were filled with survivors of Cluj, Munkacs, Oradia Mare and other towns, and the Polish survivors of Lodz and Pietrkow occupied smaller rooms. The boys wrote the names of their home towns on the bedroom doors.

Each group consisted of boys ranging from 8 to 21 years of age, the older ones taking care of the children. Little by little the fighting came to an end. Whenever a quarrel started, the friends of the antagonists would intervene and stop the disputes. A fraternal atmosphere soon developed, not only in the individual rooms, but throughout the entire group. In order to stop the hoarding of food in their bedrooms, we decided to leave the kitchen doors open all night and told the boys that they were free to help themselves to bread,

Sports meet. Theodor Lowy, Natan Swarc, Romek Wajsman, Leon Friedman, Hershel Ungar, Unidentified, Jakob Kapelusz, Beniek Mrowka, Led by Max from France

Students again. Theodor Lowy and Jakob Kapelusz

cookies, eggs and jam. Their hoarding had meant extra work for Niny and myself, as we had to collect plates and dishes throughout the house. "This is your home, everything is at your disposal" we often told them. "There is no need to take leftovers to your rooms." The food remained the most important issue and the boys were very grateful for our efforts to obtain kosher meat. They kept us company in the kitchen, "just like home." And they stopped behaving like squirrels. Most children and adolescents enjoy looking at photos of themselves and our boys were no exception. They often went to Vendome by themselves just to have their pictures taken. We asked the French railroad company to add a special car to the Thursday train, and after the weekly visit to the municipal bathhouse, we would all go to the photographer who did a tremendous business with us.

Due to the freedom and trust the children enjoyed and the religious practices observed by us, a gradual harmonious atmosphere spread throughout the house. The young people seemed calmer and more open, revealing to us a subtle image of how they must have looked before the war.

But their mentality had basically not changed. They spoke endlessly of the camps and searched the lists of survivors looking for family. The chance of finding someone grew less with each passing day, but some of the boys remained hopeful. On Yom Kippur, the Day of Atonement, cruel reality emerged. When saying the Kaddish, the prayer for the dead, they engaged in passionate discussions and disputes. Some refused to say the prayer for their parents, brothers and sisters; "They might not be dead. How awful and disgraceful to pray for them as if they were dead!" Others retorted: "But you have been in Auschwitz yourself; you have seen the gas chambers with your own eyes, and the smoke, the corpses. You witnessed what happened to the women and children. Why keep any illusions? We have to say the prayers for the dead!" In the end, some of them left the synagogue while others stayed to say Kaddish. All those I met later as adults remembered this day of Yom Kippur for it had marked the turning point in their lives. Was it pure coincidence that those who left the synagogue refusing to admit the deaths of their relatives later married French or American-born women, or Israeli women who had spent all their lives in Israel, while those who had said Kaddish, later married primarily other Holocaust survivors?

Near the end of summer at Ambloy, the group as a whole seemed to feel much better than upon arrival, but some of the boys suffered from deep depressions. One evening on the way to my room, I came across a tall, very thin young man with large, soft eyes. I had never seen him before! It was about three o'clock in the morning; he was leaning out of the window looking at the beautiful trees in the park. I asked him his name: "I do not exist," he answered, "I don't want to live any more. I don't want to see the sun, or daylight ever again. I only get up at night time to smell the wind."

I wondered how he managed to get food.

"My comrades bring me food, but I won't live much longer. Each day brings me closer to death."

I talked to him several nights in a row and little by little I found out about his childhood. He had been living in Szatmar in a warm family atmosphere. He had two older sisters and had been the only son for a long time. Later, four younger brothers and sisters were born.

It took him a long time to get interested in life again and he did not leave his room until it was time to depart from Ambloy. He learned his father's trade — printing — and is now living in Brooklyn, one of the Jewish sections of New York. He is married and has several children.

One of the most severely depressed cases was Aron, who tried several times to jump out of the window of his room. We found a room on the ground floor, for his safety. He refused to talk for many weeks. Because of his physical strength, he had been forced to work in one of the "Sonderkommandos" of Auschwitz. These inmates were in charge of carting the bodies to the crematoria. He had also been forced to carry the bodies of his dead parents and "hadn't felt anything." Now, he cannot forgive himself.

Aron lives in Israel today. He remembers having suffered from a depression in Ambloy but he has forgotten what caused it. It lies buried within, deep enough to allow him to function in daily life.

The sense of culpability of Zoltan was of a different nature and showed other effects. He was terribly thin and desperately tried to gain weight, but threw up whatever he swallowed. Before deportation he had been in love with a young girl, Edna, and they had intended to marry and move to Israel. His parents, however, disapproved and had engaged him to another girl, Myriam. His parents and Myriam died in concentration camps. The guilt over the idea that Myriam's death suited his plans to marry Edna (if she was alive) was the cause of Zoltan's illness. He physically reacted to his guilt with his body rejecting all food, and therewith the possibility of recovery.

Once his problem was analysed and understood, Zoltan was able to eat normally again. He was one of the first to leave for Israel — where Edna, not knowing Zoltan had survived, had just married someone else.

Only two of our boys actually made plans for their future. They had asked to share a room, even though one was Polish and the other Hungarian, and they prepared for university together. One of them was Kalman Kalikstein, a noted nuclear scientist in the United States and a professor at New York University. The other was Elie Wiesel, the famous author, whose works inspired worldwide remembrance of the Holocaust. He made notes for his first book, *Night*, at Ambloy.

The OSE considered Ambloy a sort of recovery home and the time had come to think about the future, to take a realistic view and to prepare for the children's integration into society. After Yom Kippur we asked each of the boys their intentions for the future. The youngest ones, who did not read or write, would have to go to school, but this prospect scared them. The idea of being separated from the group, of having to mingle with other children was frightening. Would they be accepted by others? Twelve-year old Yankel begged me not to send him to school. He feared that he could not handle it. The OSE helped us resolve the problem by creating a special class for the smallest ones so they could still be together a little longer.

When we asked the older ones what they might want to learn, the

The home at Le Vésinet

adolescents looked at Niny and me in complete bewilderment. They did not know. They did not want anything. We therefore tried a different approach, inquiring about their fathers' work. Many of them welcomed the idea of carrying on a family tradition based on their past, and decided to learn their father's trade, be it furrier, tailor, leather-maker or watchmaker.

With all that we knew and learned about our boys, we were not able to truly perceive the trauma of concentration camp life and create a picture of that trauma. For the reader's sake we offer two representative accounts through the eyes of two children — Lulek and Romek.

COMMENTARY AND DISCUSSION ON CHAPTERS 1-3

BY ROBERT KRELL AND JUDITH HEMMENDINGER

*T*he need for companionship amongst the children is a poignant contradiction to those who have written that survival was gained at the expense of others. Rather, survival depended on relationships with others, a fact which the German oppressors deliberately exploited. They tolerated neither conversation nor camaraderie, undermining any attempt for the prisoners to retain human connectedness. And yet, friendships existed, and family members tried to care for each other.

The fact that the OSE prepared 500 beds for little children reflects the failure to recognize that young children had no appreciable chance of surviving concentration camps and death marches. In fact, most were adolescents and youths.

Upon arrival at Écouis it was inevitable that fights and rivalries broke out among the various groups of children, not only by country of origin but by intensity of tradition and the hierarchy of suffering. Each thought his personal torment the worst endured, for no one yet had a perspective of the totality of the horrors inflicted, least of all the caretakers. And yet, strong groups formed.

The manner in which the groups formed themselves stands in sharp contrast to the usual concept of creating groups of same-age peers. The younger ones looked up to the older ones and accepted their leadership. They were missed so much when they left for Paris that the younger ones continued to visit them. They could not bear another loss of these older boys who were their protectors and parent substitutes. While in the camps, each youngster had behaved as if he were many years older in order to survive, but they reverted to being frightened, vulnerable and suspicious children soon after liberation.

The younger children who had bonded with the older ones and admired them were suddenly deprived of their protection and guidance when the former returned to school and the latter to work. It would have been unbearable to lose contact.

Their preoccupation with photos and being photographed likely reflects not only the wish for proof that they were alive, but to see themselves and how they looked (there were no mirrors in the camps and family photos in their possession had been destroyed) in an attempt to recapture the identity of a name combined with a vision of the person attached to it. Most had been only a number for years and bereft of a self-image, an image imprinted as uniquely one's own.

One can only speculate about the observation that those who said Kaddish later married other survivors, while those who did not married non-survivors. It is possible that those who accepted the deaths of their families and began to mourn them reconstructed family by marrying women similarly bereft. It was a union of two people, all alone, but with similar traditional upbringing and personal knowledge of wartime experiences.

Those who postponed grief and mourning, in the hope of finding lost family, delayed emotional involvement until after immigration and were more likely to meet non-survivors as potential partners. In any case, only the youths and young adults were prepared to marry in the immediate post-war years. The younger ones could not consider marriage until they settled in the countries that accepted them.

LULEK'S STORY

*H*ow were we to understand these children? How could we know what they endured? When I first offered Lulek's account (1984) he was Chief Rabbi of Nethanya. Lulek is today Ashkenazi Chief Rabbi of the State of Israel. In Israel he had become very popular through radio and television appearances, especially among the younger generation. A tall and well-groomed man who speaks in extremely polished Hebrew, the rabbi is married to the daughter of a rabbi and has eight children. His account:

> I was born twice, first biologically in June 1937 in Pietrkow, and then spiritually upon my arrival in the Holy Land on July 17, 1945, the day of Tisha B'Av. I was eight years old then. I speak of a second birth because it is hard to conceive that after experiencing Buchenwald, the long marches, the hiding and the cold, that such a little orphan could become a little boy wearing blue and white shorts, playing soccer and marbles. I had walked among the dead and had helped push carts piled high with corpses to the crematoria. And yet, the same little boy had learned to sing again and to recite the alphabet. Could I actually be the same person?
>
> When I arrived in Israel it seemed as if a barrier stood between other people and me. I only knew one person, my brother Naphtali; he had arrived here with me and, of course, I did not want to leave him.

When I asked him if he wanted to tell me more about himself, he responded:

Chief Rabbi Israel Meir Lau

No, I don't want to continue my story. At all types of ceremonies I talk about the deported people, about their sufferings and their experiences, but in general terms only. I never reveal anything about myself.... I cannot.... After Buchenwald was liberated, several people wanted to take me with them. My brother Naphtali spoke about the Holy Land, which didn't mean a thing to me. I couldn't speak a word of Hebrew or Yiddish, only Polish and a few words of Russian and German. A Russian officer called Fiedor was determined to adopt me and to take me with him to Russia. In Buchenwald he had stolen some pieces of wool and knitted earmuffs for me. When the Germans yelled hats off at roll call in assembly, my ears stayed nice and warm. He was so full of life and in much better health than Naphtali, who at age 19, was a real "Mussulman."[1] After liberation I saw Fiedor ride a horse without using a saddle at such a frightening speed that it left me in awe.

Besides Fiedor, there was also a French doctor who wanted to adopt me. He described the beauty of France and Paris to me. At the time of liberation I contracted measles and was put in quarantine on the second floor of the infirmary. My brother found a ladder, climbed through the window, wrapped me in a sheet, and took me down to line up for registration to join the Youth Aliyah.[2] They only had a few places available and had we missed this opportunity, we would have had to remain in Germany for several years. I stood in line and signed with my thumbprint, as I didn't know how to write. My brother kept telling me that Palestine was a marvellous country where only Jews lived and where we would be able to lead a wonderful life. We left Écouis on an English visa for Palestine on a legal boat, the first to arrive there after the war. Upon our arrival in Haifa, about 200 young people were standing on the bridge of the

---

1. A term applied to camp inmates who had reached a state of apathy and lethargy so great that they were considered to be "the living dead."
2. An organization devoted to assisting Jewish children who wanted to emigrate to Israel.

ship, admiring Mount Carmel and the bay. We saw Arabs working in the port wearing pants as large as bags. I had seen all kinds of uniforms but never any pants of this size and I asked a kind Jewish man why these men were wearing such funny pants. Without considering that he was addressing a child, he answered "They aren't Jews, they are Arabs. They wear those large pants in order to hide the children they have stolen, and they sell them on the market as slaves." I promptly responded: "Ich gehe nicht" (I won't go). "I didn't come here to be stolen and sold on the market. I won't leave the ship!"

At the absorption centre of Atlit, we were behind a fence once again, and stayed there for two weeks. Our names had been published in all of the newspapers and many people came to ask for news about their families who had remained in Europe. Thousands of people stood outside of the fences and called out names. One day in August, a very tall young man wearing khaki clothing, sandals and a cap on his blond hair arrived at the centre. Naphtali explained: "Lulek, there is your brother!" It was Chiko. When the war started, he had been studying in a yeshiva in Rumania. Since then, we were without news from him and feared the worst. But he had managed to escape and come to Palestine in 1944. He was a member of the Kibbutz Kfar Etzion, where some of the members had seen our names in the newspapers. Chiko, who was working in the fields at that time, dropped everything and came to us.

Two weeks later, several buses picked us up from Atlit and took us to various parts of the country according to our political beliefs. In our case of course, since I was so young, we went to the part of the country that corresponded to Naphtali's beliefs. We were sent to a children's home in Kfar Saba and had to live in barracks once more for about one month. An uncle, who was the rabbi of Katovice, Poland, found us there.

Upon his arrival in the Holy Land in 1940 with his wife and daughter, my uncle was very poor. He had become a rabbi in a small town near Haifa. He was a handsome, well-dressed man, with a beautiful grey beard like Herzl; he gave me a chocolate and socks for a present. He and Naphtali engaged in a long discussion behind closed doors during which they decided that it wasn't proper for a little boy of eight to be dragged from one home to another. Having only one daughter, 12 years of age, my uncle agreed to take me in while Naphtali attended a yeshiva at Petach Tikva. Naphtali had not told me his plans because he knew that I did not trust a soul. The only thing he said to me was "Let's go and visit our uncle. He lives in a town where people live in straw huts because they are very poor. Our uncle, however, being a rabbi, owns a beautiful wooden house."

This was his way to prepare me psychologically. When we arrived at my uncle's beautiful house I was very impressed by the blue tiles in the staircase. My aunt, my mother's sister, opened the door, deeply moved, and she kissed me and spoke to me in Polish. At least we had a common language. She had set a beautiful table and put chocolate cigarettes on a plate just for me, but I declined and said very seriously: "No, thank you, I don't smoke." Naphtali stayed for three days. Then he explained: "I will be leaving for the yeshiva and you are going to stay here." I cried bitterly — but it was to no avail. I had to get used to the idea of living with my relatives. When accompanying my aunt to the grocery store I clutched her hand for fear that she might abandon me. All the neighbours knew my story, felt sorry for me and tried to be nice to me. But I kept my distance.

Two boys, Ygal and Uri, lived in the only two storey house on our street. They wanted to play with me, but I was not very cooperative. I was quite short. I could walk under a table without bending over. When I was in the yard one day, one of the two boys, who were older than I, brought out a big, beautiful red ball. He spoke Hebrew, I spoke Polish. The ball was to be, in a way, our common tongue, but I did not want to catch it. I had never played with a ball and I was suspicious. He wouldn't give up though and when I finally agreed to catch the ball I went towards him, and standing on tiptoe, pinched his cheek as if to say "You are a nice boy."

When school started again, I found myself enrolled in first grade even though I was already 8 years old. But I could not speak Hebrew. On our first day, we learned only one word: "Shalom," "Shalom dad, Shalom mum." As noontime approached, a boat was drawn on the blackboard in honour of the new immigrant — myself. There were plenty of heads on the deck and the whole class shouted "Shalom!" I went home to my aunt and said, "I am not going back to school. The teachers make us sit for four hours just to learn one word. That's not for me." My aunt went to see the principal and he told her, "When he can count to 20 in Hebrew and understand what addition and subtraction mean, then he can be admitted into second grade."[1] My aunt taught me the very same day and the next day I was admitted into second grade. A month later I knew enough Hebrew to go into third grade and be with children my own age. But I found the daily routine of school unbearable, so different from what I had known until then. I had entered third grade four months before the end of school year. For the annual awards ceremony, the pupils made a cart used to bring in the harvest; it was for me, who had harvested so many grades in just one year.

In Buchenwald, the prisoners' numbers were not tattooed on their arms but sewn into their shirtsleeves. In other camps the numbers were tattooed on the left arm.[2] I was very humiliated when I found out that other deported persons had

---

1. In 1994, the rabbi recounted this story to us (Waisman and Krell). When his aunt described to Lulek, the conditions for his advancement, he was surprised. In the camps he had counted hundreds of corpses and he was expected to count to only twenty in Hebrew! It sounded too easy.
2. Many of the children and adolescents who were marched from Auschwitz to Buchenwald had been tattooed in Auschwitz. Those who arrived from other camps, such as Skarzysko, were not. Long-time original Buchenwald inmates had shirtsleeve numbers.

real tattoos. Nobody was going to believe that I had been in a camp! So I wrote my number on my arm with ink but it disappeared after the first bath. My pride was restored when the government had decided to give a general vaccination against typhus or smallpox. I don't remember which. Since this was very costly, they initially gave a slight vaccination. If a swelling appeared it meant that the body had had this sickness or a more serious one. I implored God to make my arm swell and it did! I was immune. I had been through great ordeals!

I never talked about the camps with my friends but they discovered that I was different from them. And there was something else. How many children mourn their father and mother at the same time? I did not know on which date my parents died but I joined the families of the deported who on the 10th of Tevet said Kaddish, a date set by rabbis as a collective day of mourning. At this occasion, the son who recites Kaddish provides at the end of the service liquor, cognac and cookies in order to remember the soul travelling to heaven. Since I wasn't able to do that, I did something else. The grocer had given me a large empty cookie box where I stored the marbles that I had won. Being 13 years old I decided that it was about time for me to be morally prepared for life at the yeshiva and that I wasn't going to continue playing with marbles like a baby. On the 10th of Tevet, I distributed all my marbles at school, explaining the reasons for my generosity. It was a rather unusual way to celebrate the ascension of my parents' souls.

I never mentioned the camps, not even to my uncle. The first time I talked in front of others was during the Eichmann trial. I was staying with my in-laws at the time; we listened to the radio broadcast of the trial, the testimonies of witnesses and Hausner's speech for the prosecution, "I am representing six million victims." As a former camp inmate, my brother Naphtali had been sent to the trial as a reporter for the newspaper "Haaretz." He, however, could not bear the stress and left

Jerusalem to stay with us for relief. It was then we exchanged memories about the camps — an unusual thing for us to do.

As a rabbi I am often invited to different commemorations on the 27th of Nissan, "Yom Hashoah,"[1] the official day for commemoration, and for the 10th of Tevet.[2] Instead of beginning with the chant "El Molei Ráchamim" (God of mercy), I usually ask for the particular commemoration book of that community and read a few excerpts. When I talk in schools, children are quick to realise that I am not just speaking as a rabbi, but that I am personally involved. I usually relate not only the facts of which everyone is aware by now, but I also talk about the emotions they stir up. I refuse to accept the tribute paid to the resistance fighters' bravery and courage, as if the others had not also been heroes.

In the evenings, my father-in-law would read a chapter about a community which disappeared in order to accomplish the commandment of the Torah: "Remember Amalek."[3] My father-in-law, Rav Yzhok-Yedidia Frenkel, Chief Rabbi of Tel Aviv, is an extraordinary man who I met at the yeshiva long before I married his daughter. The first time I saw her in Bnei Brak, I wanted to marry her, but did not call on her father then. I did not meet her again for six months. After having found work at my old yeshiva in Jerusalem, I called her brother, explaining to him that while I knew that the father usually made the request for his son, I could not abide by the custom for I was an orphan. I was finally permitted to make a date with the young girl. We saw each other frequently and secretly became engaged. I still had not met her father, the rabbi, but in the end he agreed to see me at his house on a Saturday evening after the Sabbath.

---

1. The day of the catastrophe. The official day of remembrance for Holocaust victims.
2. The fast which marks the beginning of the siege of Jerusalem by Nebuchadnezzar.
3. The people of Amalek attacked the people of Israel in the desert, beginning with the sick and weak ones. Amalek represents the evil no one should ever forget.

He was alone and served me an excellent dinner. Then he spoke to me. "After three sons, God blessed us with a girl. My wife and I love her dearly. I was told that you are a very talented student, but I must be honest with you and will explain the reasons why I hesitated to give my only daughter to a man who is alone in the world, who never had a family life and does not remember his parents. How can such a man raise a family? Will he make our daughter happy? I would like to cite a verse of the Torah: For this (marriage), a man will leave his father and mother (Genesis II, 24). I won't translate the word 'azav' literally with 'leave,' but rather with the word 'izavon,' which has the same root and meaning as 'heritage.' I believe that because of her education, our daughter has what is needed to create the basis for a solid and genuine Jewish family, and I trust you to make her happy." From that day on my life has been different. I am received like a son in the rabbi's family and my wife and I now have eight children.

Today, all eight children are married. His three sons and five sons-in-law are rabbis in Israel. One son together with a son-in-law created two large yeshivot (Talmudic Colleges), one in Nethanya, the other in Jerusalem, in memory of both their grandfathers. All the children are committed to continue the tradition of their parents and grandparents.

ROMEK'S STORY

Now known as Robbie Waisman, businessman, family man and active teacher of children about the Holocaust and its implications, Robbie looks 15 years younger than his chronological age. His winning personality and perpetual optimism conceal the struggle with memories of his complicated past. And yet, by offering his memories to thousands of school children, he has healed parts of himself and achieved some measure of peace and accomplishment. His account:

Although my years with my family were few, I shall never forget the warmth of my home. I was the youngest. My older sister and four older brothers were active in Zionist youth organisations. I remember the Shabbats, the Yomim Tovim (High Holy Days), my father's Tallith (prayer shawl) wrapped around him and me as well. I felt as secure and completely protected as a child could feel. I was 8 years old when the Germans occupied Skarczysko and we were forced to work in the munitions factory. My father and I were witness to the brutal murder of my brother Avram, only three years older than I. After his death, my father's black hair turned white. His strength was gone. I needed him. I became angry with him for not being strong enough to look after me anymore. I did not appreciate his pain. Now as a father myself, I understand it and I am ashamed when I think of my anger.

I worked for a year and a half in the factory and survived many "selections." When the family was finally separated and I lost sight of my brothers and father, I befriended another little

Robert Waisman (photo by Myron Unrau)

boy, Abram Czapnik, who was 11 months younger. We went through the rest of the war together. We were inseparable. Without his friendship I would have lost my bearings and perished. Perhaps he would say the same about me. One day a trainload of potatoes was dumped in an open area. It was too late to store them so they were guarded by two soldiers who marched around the giant pile. We were starving, as usual, and counted the precise times the guards disappeared from view as they circled. I volunteered to run and steal some potatoes. Failure meant certain death. Abram argued that he was faster and made a precision-timed dash, undetected. As with everything, we shared the bounty.

We were transferred to Buchenwald in 1944 and Abram and I were placed in a barracks with Polish, French and German political prisoners who protected us.[1] Throughout my stay in Buchenwald I thought that my oldest brothers would survive, they were so big, so strong and I was so little and so weak. I wanted to show them, to surprise them. I wanted to make it too.

But shortly after April 11, 1945, when I was 14 years old, I discovered that only my sister Leah and I had survived. Two months later, we children were still in Buchenwald. Our homes were gone and finally 430 of us were accepted into France. We arrived in a small village called Écouis, run by the OSE — a children's rescue society. To their horror, they discovered quickly that we were unusual to say the least, a horde of suspicious, distrusting, rebellious and hostile children — as if from some other planet. They tried to give us salad to eat. Did we survive to be fed like rabbits? Then they gave us smelly Camembert cheese. Why were we given food that smelled foul to us, as if it should be thrown away?

We learned over time to appreciate these delicacies.

---

1. Romek and Abram in Block 8 were unaware that Block 66 held the children. At liberation they thought themselves the only two children in Buchenwald.

Then we were tested physically and psychologically and pronounced beyond redemption. It was at Écouis we were told we would not recover. We were said to be cold and indifferent. Some professionals believed we were true psychopaths. In a sense, were they not correct? How do you react to watching humanity and humans destroyed before your eyes, to losing all your family and friends? It was not easy to become human again. People said that we were "les enfants terribles de Buchenwald" and not redeemable.

The first time I was asked my name I blurted out my concentration camp number. No, it is your name we want. It was the first time in years that I realised I had a name.

One day I just sat down with an awareness of having lost everything, that there's no one left. That was the first time I cried. We all started questioning the existence of God. How could this happen to us? So we no longer believed in God and many of us brushed religion aside, did not ask for kosher food and we no longer prayed. We started living an agnostic life.

At first we were very eager to talk about the camp years. But no one was willing to listen; no one seemed to care what our problems were. We were told by professional experts to forget the past. We now know that this was a mistake. Back then psychiatry did not know about the severe trauma of the Holocaust. We all had to find our own ways in dealing with our pain and the loss of loved ones. Écouis was pivotal for us, a sobering place, a return to the real world. We had to come to terms with what we were doing and where we were going.

Social workers who tried to help us were wonderful, but had no idea what to do with us. An expert was brought to talk to us. We drowned him out by continuing our own conversations. He was furious. He took off his jacket and it looked like he wanted to hit us. As he rolled up his sleeve, we saw his Auschwitz number tattooed on his arm. A hush fell over the crowd. There was a long pause. He did not speak. After several minutes all he

managed to say was "Meine tyre kindern" (my dear children)
and began to cry. We cried with him. For many it was the first
time.

From Écouis I went to Vésinet with about 50 Buchenwald
boys to join about 50 French Jewish orphans. We were
integrated into the school system. The older boys went to Paris.
It was a sad development for us younger ones. When we
realised we had no parents, we began to look to them as parent
substitutes, our protectors. We missed them so much. It was
another great loss. That is why we continued to visit them. Only
a very few found relatives and several moved to the United
States. How we envied them. I could not seek advice from my
contemporaries. When the hope of returning home to family
evaporated, and the older boys were moved, I felt so alone and
so vulnerable. After years of behaving as if I were an adult, I
was a child again.

At first it was acceptable to be a 'Déporté' but that didn't last
long. We wanted to learn French as quickly and flawlessly as
possible. We wanted to be like other French children. I was at
Vésinet through 1946-1948 and caught up to my age group at
school.

A wonderful man, Professor Manfred Reingwitz, a teacher of
French and German at the Sorbonne, helped us with our lessons
at night. Our Director was a man named Fisch. In the summer
he arranged for us to go to Champigny-sur-Marne, another
home just for the summer, but where we continued our
education. Learning was wonderful for it left no time to think of
the past. Judith was at Taverny, a home where other boys went,
similar to Vésinet.

I was in France when I discovered my sister had survived the
camps. She married another survivor and moved to Palestine. I
tried to get to Palestine but the plans fell through and I certainly
did not want to stay in Europe. I wanted to leave all that
reminded me of the horrors, as far away as I could. France was

too close to Germany. It was too close to the pain that we suffered, and I thought that by leaving I would completely obliterate those memories. I was wrong. You cannot run away from yourself. Those memories do stay with you. The two places that we picked were Canada (we heard it was a wonderful country) and a lot of us thought Australia would be even better because it took three months to get there at that time, so that's far enough! I heard that Canada had opened its doors for a thousand children. I was one of the last to leave in December of 1949. At first I was rejected because of my blood count and very low blood pressure, so the doctors thought that there was something wrong with me. You had to be a very healthy specimen. Canada wasn't very liberal in its outlook towards refugees.[1] I knew it was a young country, full of opportunity and that no one there ever went hungry. And that fact played an important part in my choice. In the camps we used to fantasize of having enough bread and butter and the idea that food was available to anybody who wanted to work played a big part in our decision-making.

I wanted to go to Montreal and I kicked up a fuss when they sent me out West, because I thought if I went to Montreal I wouldn't have to learn English. I already spoke French. So I said, if I can't go to Montreal I want to go to Toronto. And they said no, you can't go to Toronto. Well, OK then I want to go to Vancouver. And they agreed to send me there. En route to Vancouver, Mrs. Pearlman, the social worker who picked us up in Halifax, told us we were stopping in Calgary for a few days because the place in Vancouver was not quite ready. This was actually a trick because they never intended for us to go to Vancouver. So we stopped in Calgary and I stayed.

---

1. For pre-war Canada's response to Jewish refugees, see "None is Too Many" by Irving Abella and Harold Troper, Toronto: Lester and Orpen Dennys Ltd., 1982. Canada's post-war acceptance of over 1,000 Jewish children is described by Ben Lappin in "Redeemed Children," Toronto, Canada: University of Toronto Press, 1963, and by Fraidie Martz in "Open Your Hearts," Véhicule, 1996.

I arrived in Calgary on a Tuesday, was placed in the home of Harry and Rachel Goresht and their children, Ida, and Sam, and Wednesday morning I went to work. I just wanted to become a normal human being, pursue a career and make a life for myself. We survivors enjoyed quite a nice reputation in Calgary. We became friends with the community. If there was a wedding, we either got invited to the wedding or at least to the reception. So we were always there for the dances. The Goresht's daughter, Ida would introduce me as her brother. It was good to be surrounded by all this affection and I have a strong bond with my foster family still today.

A young Edward Bronfman lived in Calgary at that time. He was there to look after the Royalite Gas Company. He had a convertible car (DeSoto). We used to chum around together. He gave us rides and he'd treat in the restaurants. It was great! Calgary was absolutely wonderful. There was a warmth that is very, very hard to describe. We were included in everything. We did everything. It was a fun time, and it was healing. The Jewish community certainly made an effort. They were there for us. But we handled our emotional problems ourselves and if we couldn't handle them, we just ended up sick. Our crying was done within, on our own time, by ourselves. I think we still do this. From what we know today, we probably needed counselling. We did it the hard way. On our own. The camaraderie and the closeness among survivors in Calgary played a large part in the healing process.

There was one orphan, Jack, who was in Calgary with me, and he couldn't cope. He was unable to adapt and he was admitted to the asylum. He had his fingers shot off in one of the camps. He had depressive moods and I felt an attachment to him and tried to help him. We thought we'd be able to get him out and we used to visit every Sunday.

We'd go and talk to him and he'd put his foot up right over his head and he would talk and look funny and then he would talk about the camps and all that happened, but not in a normal way. Later they wouldn't let us in because he was often in a straight jacket and under sedation. After a while he didn't know us. I don't know what happened to him. He just gave up.

One of the Calgary group, Aron Eichler, married in 1954 to Ida Zysblat, and the rest of us in Calgary would get together almost daily at their home. They established a kind of extended family. We practised our English and discussed our problems.

Some families were suspicious of the "orphans." Twice I dated girls from two separate families who of course did not have an opportunity to get to know me. Nevertheless, when the relationships progressed they put a stop to it. I was a bit angry but I had my pride. Anybody who did not want me, no big deal, I did not want them either. And love hadn't gone so far that I was heartbroken. I married a girl from a very prominent family in Saskatoon, Gloria Lyons. When I was dating Gloria, they looked into my personal history. My wife was warned she was marrying someone from a completely different background who had gone through the war. So there was discouragement. Not many of us were integrated to a degree where they were dating Canadian-born women. As far as I was concerned, I was simply looking for the right person.

I sometimes think that to have been a child survivor was much easier than to have been an adult survivor. Perhaps we didn't think as deeply as an adult, for now when I put myself in my father's shoes, I understand why his black curly hair turned white in a period of two weeks. My father was a leader in our town, very well respected in the community. His counsel and advice were sought by friends and neighbours. His positive views and attitude were always welcomed. He was deeply in love with his wife, Rifkele, and this love carried over to all of his children. My father kept everyone's outlook bright during the start of the war. He used to laud the accomplishments of

Germany's writers, scientists and musicians. His strong belief in that civilized society must have devastated him when it all fell apart during the Holocaust. I understood much later about his pain. As an adult, he had a better understanding of the situation and probably already knew that his wife went to Treblinka. He also had other loved ones whom he lost. That knowledge must have been completely devastating and he probably gave up at this point in time. I did not know and just thought of myself and the will to survive. My father kept details from me and I was angry with him because I needed his strength and it was not there anymore. I was already 12 years old and should have known better. Now that anger has come back to haunt me. Now I am angry with myself that I did not have more compassion towards my father.

I became an accountant and moved to Saskatoon in 1959 where I opened a clothing store and devoted myself to Jewish community work. I served as President of the B'nai B'rith and then as President of the Saskatoon Jewish community. Few persons in Saskatoon knew I was a survivor.

In the 1970's I attended a wedding in Toronto. A man originally from Skarzysko heard the name of Waisman and came over to speak to me. He knew my family. He could not believe I was the youngest son. He told me he was a friend of my older brother and remembered me as a little child. He gave me some details of my brother's murder. I was devastated. But I wanted to know. I had hoped that my older brother was alive somewhere in Russia because he had served in the Polish army. He was like a James Bond to me. I looked up to him and I thought nothing could ever, ever harm him. To me, he was invincible. But I guess he wasn't.

I put my past aside. I raised a family and they knew very little about my experiences. My wife knew about my background, but people in Saskatoon were shocked when I first started talking. I was having flashbacks from the camps. In the camps were philosophers and writers among the Jewish prisoners and I heard their discussions. I remember one person turning to me and saying, "Anybody who survives this war, he will live in paradise and everything is going to be perfect. There will be no racism, and no anti-Semitism, and finally people will have learned to live with one another." Then another turned to me and said "Hey, you punk, come over here. If you survive, if you happen to survive, you must tell people what you've seen and heard and how bad it was and what the Nazis did. Remember that." Well, it sort of went in one ear and out the other. That conversation flashed back and I felt, particularly after Keegstra,[1] that I have a responsibility and a duty to talk. And survivors are dying out, I am the baby of the survivors and I'm in my sixties. Time is running out, and we have to do everything possible to warn others so it doesn't repeat itself. I have a strong urgency to do as much as I possibly can. And I want to be sure the deaths of our loved ones were not in vain. So I speak to kids, young students, about the Holocaust.

When I read "None is Too Many" I had to put it down several times because I was so angry about what had happened. I like to think that the despicable conduct of people like Prime Minister Mackenzie King and Frederick Blair, who was the Director of Immigration, has influenced the present government to become more humane and that Canada agreed to open its doors for the boat people from Cambodia because they were facing a similar fate. I like to believe in my heart that it's a result of the disgusting manner in which some leaders behaved towards the innocent Jewish children from Europe.

We moved to Vancouver in 1978 and I have been involved in both the Jewish and general community. The main change is that since 1983 I have been active in the Vancouver Holocaust Centre Society, as Treasurer, Vice-President and President. After

---

1. The Keegstra trial in Alberta in 1983 took place after this teacher was exposed as having taught high school students Jewish conspiracy theories and Holocaust denial for 13 years.

decades of suppressing my past, I now promote Holocaust awareness and education with all my being.

I have led a normal adult life, married and raised two children. In my mind, normality and surviving the Holocaust are two different things. When you really think about what survivors experienced, how can we be normal. It is true. Some of the thoughts and some of the ways we think cannot be normal. And yet, no one should feel sorry for me. I do not need sympathy. No one should say "poor Robbie, what you must have gone through." I don't want this. We have proven to ourselves that we're normal human beings, that we have raised families and become responsible members of the community. We have made many productive contributions and now, later in life, can look back and say, the Holocaust occurred, this is what happened and these are the things we must do so that it does not happen again.

I was told by my teacher, Professor Manfred Reingwitz who really took a liking to me, "If you keep on with the pain it will surely destroy you." He went on to say "You must learn to put it aside, go back to school and concentrate on your future." Most of the boys finally accepted this advice and we started on our way back to becoming normal human beings. It was not easy. Looking back, I can tell you that you cannot escape the past. Memories, particularly the bad ones are always ready to spring up at you. A railroad crossing, a smell, a word, any number of situations brings back horrors. Memories — a song can do it for normal people. For us, it is sirens and dogs barking. Still, for more than 30 years I did not talk about my experiences in the camps.

Upon arrival to Canada, we remained silent in order to appear normal. We went to dances and we played poker. We did not talk of the horrors. But we survivors continued to nourish each other and do so to this day. People must have thought "There go the children who became old before they were children." Indeed, if we had become savages, no one could have blamed us. Instead, somehow we have managed to become good people and good citizens, even though we were robbed of our childhood.

6

TAVERNY

*H*alfway between Paris and Enghien, the train stopped at the little station of Taverny. The castle of Vaucelles, in Taverny, a large property lying in the middle of a park, was to be the new home for the boys, Niny, and myself. It had been requisitioned by the Germans during the war. Our first task was to remove the heavy iron gate which they had erected for protection.

The boys were free to decide which dormitory or room they wanted to move into and who they wanted to sit with in the dining room. During the two years in Taverny, none of them changed their initial seating places. Recently I met a former "child of Taverny" and described the place he had occupied in the dining room. He remarked "of course, it was the one closest to the kitchen!"

The younger ones were sent to Jewish vocational school, the ORT,[1] then located in the Rue des Saules near Montmartre. I once had to go to Paris on an errand and was among the latecomers. The train had already started to move and some of the boys raced after it, trying to jump on. I saw them fall to the ground and thought the train had run over them. When the last train was gone and when I could see them get back to their feet, I fainted from shock. The two, who had been left behind, had to carry me home. When the others returned that evening, all of them came to visit me in my room. The fact that I was so concerned about their fate, and fainted over the possibility that something could have happened to them, overwhelmed them. They could not yet imagine that someone cared about them being alive.

In addition to their studies and schooling, the boys were expected to help with the chores in the house and preparing for Shabbat. At first they refused, having worked so hard in the camps they felt deserving of being looked after. However, they readily agreed to prepare for Shabbat, for such preparations

---

1. ORT — Organization for Educational Resources and Technological Training.

Le Chateau Vaucelles at Taverny

reminded them of home. The little ones of the OSE school also pitched in, for they wanted to be with their "brothers." Together, we prepared for the Jewish holidays, each boy having an assigned task.

The two oldest boys led the Jewish traditional life in the spirit of their vanished communities. Meyer-Tzvi, who descended from a line of extraordinary Rabbis, was the spiritual head and was respected by everyone. Moshe, a strong, healthy boy and well-spoken leader, prepared the ceremonies. He felt responsible for the religious behaviour of his comrades.

I had been absent during one Shabbat and when I returned home Sunday morning, I sensed an unusual tension throughout the house. The boys told me what had happened. As usual, a warm and peaceful atmosphere had spread throughout the house, when suddenly Shlomo walked in dressed in work clothes. There was no doubt that he had taken the train from Paris even though travelling was forbidden during Shabbat. All eyes were on him when Moshe silently stood up, walked over to Shlomo and slapped his face. Niny, furious with such behaviour, left the room without saying a word. The joy of that Shabbat had been shattered.

The Directors of other homes also housing children from Buchenwald had been selected according to their ability to command authority. They envied us for they could not understand why our liberal methods were so successful. But one of our boys, Simon, found the religious life of Taverny in the Vaucelles hostel far too strict and on a Monday morning decided to go to another home, Le Vésinet. He was back by Tuesday evening and we accepted him without asking questions.

Approximately 25 years later I happened to meet the former Director of Le Vésinet. When he learned that Simon was now living in the United States with his family, he exclaimed: "That's impossible! The boy is crazy and must make his family very unhappy." He recalled that "Simon arrived at Le Vésinet one evening at 9.00 o'clock and declared that he was hungry. I told him that, unfortunately, dinner in our house was served at 7.00 o'clock and that breakfast would be the next meal. He replied that clearly I had not understood him, that

Group Instruction.

Manfred Reingwitz teaching

Students and teachers. Manfred Reingwitz, Romek Wajsman,
Salek Finkelstein, Manfred Lewin.

he was hungry <u>now</u>. I quietly explained to him that we were running an orderly home and that everything was cleared away after meals and that he could not eat before the next morning. He then stormed into the kitchen, breaking the locked kitchen door with his shoulders, opened the cupboards and like a maniac threw all the dishes onto the floor. Naturally, I sent him back."

We were very fortunate to receive help through the exceptional influence of Leo Margulies, who had been a leader of a Jewish youth organisation before the war and was deported to Buchenwald in 1939. When the camp was liberated, he insisted on looking after the children of Barracks 66, accompanying them on their journey to France. They trusted him and admired him for having survived six years in Buchenwald. He was on excellent terms with the boys. However, the OSE considered him too old to stay in a children's home and sent him to Paris. But the children of Écouis trusted only "Monsieur" Margulies, a fellow camp inmate like them and who knew what they had suffered. He was permitted to return and became their spokesman in all matters of management. Leo Margulies was an honest, religiously observant individual and for him, the children behaved properly without need for drastic measures in order to have them comply with expectations.

A younger leader was Michel who arrived one day at Taverny and told us "My parents were arrested in Paris, but I was able to go into hiding and my life was spared. I am not yet prepared to lead a normal life and would very much like to help take care of the young deported children, if you will have me."

He was about 20 years old at the time and wore shorts and had a crew cut. His bright eyes and resolute air quickly won the boys' hearts. They were amazed to find out that he was a vegetarian to whom food was not all that important. Once, when all except Michel suffered food poisoning from eating spoiled fish, they were astonished. Michel seldom spoke. When he did, it was profoundly effective, no words were wasted. Once he saw the boys pulling the legs off a fly and simply asked, "Why would you do such a thing?" To this day the boys remember how deeply ashamed they felt at this question stated without reproach. Michel did exercises with the boys each morning. They became proud of their increased strength and their growing muscles. Being strong, kind, tolerant and using authority without abusing it, Michel had a very positive influence on them. He served as an example and helped many of them adjust to

Judith and some of the boys

Niny and some of the boys

the requirements of their new life. Even now, when I meet a former alumnus of Taverny, his first question is "Do you know what happened to Michel?" "Yes," I tell them, "Michel is now living in Beer-Sheva, Israel, and he is a pacifist who refuses to carry arms. He is still youthful in appearance, and wears his shorts in summer and winter. He has remained a vegetarian and devotes his life and energy to his community."

Seventeen-year-old Israel arrived at Taverny much later. He was a high school graduate from Israel who wanted to become a pianist and had registered at the Paris Conservatory. Because of his piano playing, he was unable to find a room. He had heard about us and decided to ask if he could rent a room in Taverny. I offered him the floor above the stables if in return he gave a concert for us on Wednesdays.

Israel immediately set to work, replastering and whitewashing the damaged walls of his room. "In the Holy Land," he said, "a Jew has to know how to do everything." When the boys discovered his talent at the piano was even greater than his plastering ability, their admiration for him knew no bounds. For them, Israel represented the new Jewish generation. They came to his Wednesday evening concerts, some sitting on the floor, and listened to him talk about Bach's melodies and their recurring themes. Then he played for them. The week after, it was Beethoven and his symphonies, then Mozart and his operas. I had bought tickets for all of us in the first row of the balcony at the Paris Opera where we saw "The Magic Flute." On the train back to Taverny, when I saw the children's happy and dreamy looks, I was grateful that fate had sent Israel to us.

One would have expected that boys of their age, many already learning a trade, would feel tempted to leave the home and begin to lead an independent life. Quite the contrary. Whenever a boy met another survivor from his home country, he would ask him to come to the house, although it was already quite full. The boys also wanted to invite their friends for Shabbat. Inclusion of a guest to Taverny for Shabbat was determined by a simple criterion: "Do you believe that your parents would have invited him?" thereby leaving the decision in their hands.

We of course never refused a brother or sister who showed up at Taverny. One day, two young girls clad in rags, their feet wrapped in pieces of cloth, came to Taverny looking for their brother, Icu Gluck. The younger of the two, Lilly,

The studious ones with Elie Wiesel in the middle

gave us an account of their harrowing journey. The two sisters after liberation had returned to their home in Hungary hoping that a family member would have survived. In November of 1945 they received a telegram from the Red Cross informing them that their brother, Icu, was living in France. Upon receiving a letter from Icu who was then in Ambloy, they decided to leave for France by illegally crossing the Iron Curtain. Arriving in Paris and on a train for Ambloy, they travelled many more hours and dragged themselves from the station to the home arriving there late at night. The young girl who opened the door looked at Icu's picture and told them they were too late, but not to be afraid. Icu is alive, but living in Taverny. She explained to them how to get there and they spent the night in the waiting room at the station. The next morning at the Gare du Nord, they showed Icu's picture to a young man wearing a beret. He said that he knew Icu very well because they lived in the same children's home.

The joy of their reunion was overwhelming and it was then that Icu related the sad story of their father. Icu had been liberated from Buchenwald with his father, who was extremely weak. They went to France on foot and in American trucks. But on arrival at Mulhouse, Icu was so ill that he had to be taken to a hospital which had just reopened. The doctors told his father that his son would die without a blood transfusion, but that they had no blood reserves. His father insisted they take his blood for his son. They were placed on two beds side by side and while Icu regained his strength and returned to life, his father contracted jaundice and died. After two weeks in the hospital, not knowing where to go, Icu returned to Buchenwald to join his comrades of Barracks 66.

The two sisters adjusted very well to life in Taverny. Maggie learned to be a seamstress at the ORT and Lilly registered at the Sorbonne. Soon after, two more young girls arrived at Taverny and they also took sewing courses at the ORT. They all recovered quickly and looked healthy and beautiful again. They were admired by all the boys when they came to dinner on Friday evenings in their new self-made dresses. They had become like sisters to everyone. It was too good to last, and sure enough, one day we received a letter from the OSE in Paris stating, "We have learned that four young girls are living among your boys. This is against the rules. We have reserved four places in one of our homes in Versailles. Organise their immediate transfer."

The girls showed no reaction whatsoever to the news and one morning I accompanied them to Versailles. Not a word was spoken during the entire trip. The Director of Versailles invited us for lunch where I sat across from the four girls with tears streaming down their faces throughout the meal. After dessert, I asked them if they had unpacked. Silently they shook their heads. I then told them, "Go fetch your suitcases, we are going home."

Many years later the girls told me that leaving Taverny felt like a death sentence. They had just begun to re-learn trusting people.

Maggie and Lilly have married camp survivors and are now living in the southern United States. Lilly, with the help of her husband, founded a dress factory. She became an active member of the Jewish community and a participant in women's clubs. But she still remained lonely, and felt she had little in common with these American-born women whose concerns seemed to her futile and irrelevant.

A few years ago she finally found the courage to tell her husband about her terrible nightmares, the war memories which haunted her dreams. "Since I am unable to talk about it, I think I would like to write a book about what I have been through," Lilly said. She and her sister decided to retrace their long journey from their hometown to Auschwitz. They recognised everything; even the odours were still there, unchanged. The two sisters also visited their father's grave in the old Jewish cemetery of Zillesheim near Mulhouse. They then came to see me in Israel and we talked about Taverny. Upon her return to the United States, Lilly published her autobiography and felt relieved of a terrible burden.[1] Lilly is the mother of four children: two sons were brilliant students and an exceptionally beautiful daughter won first prize at a beauty contest in North Carolina. At a press interview she explained: "I entered the contest because of my parents' experiences. My mother always told me I was meant to live two lives, one for myself and one to make up for all the things she had missed when she was young."

Nothing could hold back any of the boys at Taverny when they learned that a family member might still be alive. They would start an immediate search. When they returned, discouraged, no one asked any questions because their silent faces spoke volumes.

---

1. Lerner, Lilly (Gluck) "The Silence," New York: Lyle Stuart Publishing Inc., 1980.

The boys grow up

*Front: Abram Gzapnik, Herchel Unger
Back: Joseph Fachler, Leon Friedman,
Marek Lozinski, Salek Sandowski, Romek
Wajsman*

*Israel Unikowski , Hersh Simon,
Romek Wajsman, Abram Gzapnik*

*Back: Romek Wajsman, Heersh Linger,
Leon Friedman
Front: Beniek Mrowka, Abram Gzapnik*

*Top row: Joseph
Fachler, Leon
Friedman, Jakob
Kapelusz, Joseph
Dziubak
Front: Visitor from
Girls' home, Idel
Goldblum*

*Top row : Joseph
Fachler, Leon
Friedman, Nathan
Laufer, Jakob
Kapelusz.
Front: Herch Simon,
Ludwig Herskovitz,
Idel Goldblum
(George Goldbloom),
Marek Lozinski*

*December 1946: Top
Row: Jakob Kapelusz
(Jerry Kapelus)
Salomon Majer (Joe
Majer), Max Kozuch,
Fajwen Kaner (Philip
Kanner)
Front Row: Wolf
Vogel (Willy Fogel)
Elias Balter (Eddy
Balter) Theodor Lowy
(Bubby Levy)*

Occasionally, they met with success. Aron, more or less recovered from his depressions, was working at the ORT school when he learned that his younger brother Uri was living in a children's home in the Black Forest of Germany. He went there immediately and returned after six long weeks with the following story. "I arrived there, found the home, and recognised my little 12-year-old brother. He yelled, 'Go away! I don't want to see you, you are dead to me. I became used to the idea that I am alone in the world and that my parents are dead and that everybody is dead. I don't want to dream any longer.'"

Aron slept outside and waited until 10.00 o'clock on the following day when the children were taken for a walk. Aron walked alongside Uri without speaking a word. When Uri returned to the home Aron stayed outside again and waited. He did this for a month. One morning, Uri said to him, "All right, I accept that you are alive and that you are my brother. Soon we will leave for Israel, come and join me there."

The home continued to be a haven of brotherhood and safety. Yet the children were becoming aware that they could not spend the rest of their lives at Taverny and that they would have to overcome their fear of the future and find individual pursuits. They often endured great trials and tribulations in order to succeed.

Two of our boys, who had decided to join their families in the United States, called us one Friday from the Consulate in Paris. They had missed the last train before the beginning of Shabbat. I told them to catch the next train to Versailles and announced their imminent arrival to the Director of that home. Upon their arrival at the station of Versailles, they asked for directions to the castle. They were sent to the Château de Versailles and searched from top to bottom without finding any of the child survivors. One of the attendants explained to them that there was a much smaller castle and how to find it. When they returned to Taverny and I asked them whether the Château de Versailles had not seemed a bit too grandiose to be a home for children, their innocent response was "not at all!" Clearly, reality was going to be a great shock for them.

Commentary and Discussion on Chapters 4-6

by Robert Krell and Judith Hemmendinger

*T*he monstrous childhood experiences of Lulek and Romek are typical of the cruelties endured by Jewish youngsters. Their narrow escapes on so many occasions accentuate the part fate played in their survival. A child could make a thousand correct decisions, and then a single error would bring death. And yet, one cannot underestimate the intelligence and wherewithal, the will and courage of these young survivors. They did themselves contribute to their long streak of luck and showed an uncanny capacity to "read" situations. Overnight they became adults, childhood was abandoned.

Rabbi Lau has described his encounter at liberation with Rabbi Hershel Schachter, a U.S. Army Chaplain. I heard it told by the rabbi on his visit to Vancouver in 1994.

> I want to share with you some experiences, starting with April 11, the day of our liberation from Buchenwald. I speak not of April 11, 1945, now, but of April 11, 1983, in Washington, D.C. at the Second World Gathering of Holocaust survivors. I was then Chief Rabbi of Nethanya and invited to come as the youngest survivor of Buchenwald on the day of liberation. They had arranged for me a meeting with Rabbi Herschel Schachter, a liberator.
>
> From 1945 to 1983 I had carried with me a memory which I thought was my imagination until I had it confirmed at the Gathering by Rabbi Schachter.
>
> Rabbi Schachter was in the first jeep to enter the gates of Buchenwald. The Germans had gone, the gates were still closed,

and there was a pile of corpses near the gates. I stayed behind the pile of bodies. The gate was broken down and the jeep entered. Rabbi Schachter was frightened, he could not believe his eyes. He saw eyes watching him, took out his gun and walked around the corpses, where he discovered a little boy with not even one tooth. He understood this must be a Jewish child and gathered me into his arms. Now I was afraid. He was a man in a uniform with a gun. For six years I had seen the uniforms of the SS, the Wehrmacht, of Einsatzgruppen. He saw how frightened I was. First he wept, then he smiled and asked in Yiddish for my name. "Lulek, in Polish they call me Lulek." He said, "How old are you, Lulek?" I would not have believed it if Rabbi Schachter had not told me this. He was a soldier, a rabbi and I was less than eight years old and yet I said, "I am older than you." So he asked why I thought so. I answered "Because you behave like a child. I haven't laughed or cried for years. I am too strong, too tough. I don't cry any more. So tell me who is older, me or you?"

It is apparent that these children knew they had grown old before their time.

While Lulek regained his name, for a time he longed for a number. Not having been tattooed, he felt other camp survivors would not believe he had been in a camp. It took many years for him to speak publicly about his experiences, the stimulus being the Eichman trial in 1961. For Romek it was not possible to speak of his nightmare years in a variety of camps until 1983 when a Holocaust denier aroused in him the need to bear witness.

Neither Rabbi Lau nor Robert Waisman have stopped speaking for they, like others, realise the importance of remembering. It does appear that memory needed to be set aside for a time, in order to get on with life. And both survivors, on the one hand, received much support, on the other, were viewed by the families of prospective brides with a degree of suspicion. Could they, after such horrendous losses, and deprived of childhood and parenting, themselves become decent husbands and good fathers?

Taverny was the site where many children began the slow and painful process of re-integrating into a society where decency and respectfulness were paramount. The Buchenwald arrivals simply could not imagine that anyone cared. A powerful connection was made to the memories of Shabbat and recollections of family life. It required the leadership of an older survivor to whom the younger camp survivors could relate to instill a sense of trust. Sports and music were available. Every day was filled with hope and despair, of longed-for reunions that did not materialise and the complexities of those that did. The homes served as an oasis of comparative calm between 1945-1947; the major tasks of returning to school, finding work, emigrating, learning languages, all still to come.

Taverny was a place of necessary transition.[1] As Jacob, eight years old at liberation and now a psychoanalyst in Paris, stated, "I think that a child survivor was a disturbed child and the family who would have agreed to take such a child would have seen in him a very disturbed child." Listing some of the strange behaviours concerning food and cleanliness issues, he continues, "Psychiatrists would have said they are really mad, insane, but in fact it was a transitory madness, a sort of behaviour madness. I think to be together in a society where everybody is like that assured us, on the contrary, a better readaptation than a family life."

A Polish boy, 16 at liberation, said, "In Taverny I felt well. I think I would not have been able to be released immediately after the camps into the free world." A further comment "Taverny also helped me to accept the fact that I am alone. There was not just one orphan who cried after his father and mother, there were a hundred teenagers, alone on earth. That shared pain was a sort of comfort."

Taverny provided a surrogate family, one that still exists. A strong sense of brotherhood links the Buchenwald—Taverny group to this day.

---

1. Judith Hemmendinger (1980). Readjustment of young concentration camp survivors through a surrogate family experience. Interaction: A Journal of the Psychiatric Institutes of America (3)3:127-134.

7

DESTINATIONS —
LEAVING TAVERNY

*I*n the immediate post-war years, the Red Cross and all important Jewish organisations published lists of survivors and among them also the names of our boys. In this way, some found relatives who insisted the youngsters should join them.

Kalman

Kalman was the first to leave Taverny for a new life in Bolivia. His was a tortuous odyssey. He had found two older brothers living in Bolivia since 1939. They had arranged for Kalman's visa and were anxious to have him join them. We informed a Jewish organisation in charge of emigration, which promised to take care of all necessary paperwork.

Like his comrades, Kalman trusted only his own eyes. After making enquiries in Paris he told us that there was no Bolivian Consulate in France. We called the immigration organisation who claimed that Kalman, who did not speak French or English, had misunderstood. They insisted that of course there was a Bolivian Consulate in Paris and requested patience while the work proceeded. Kalman showed us guides and telephone books to prove that Bolivia was not listed.

Another letter arrived from Kalman's brothers. The visa was no longer valid, but they had succeeded in obtaining a six-month extension. They warned Kalman that the trip from Paris to Lisbon and the subsequent six-week journey by ship had to be concluded within this time period.

During this time, Niny accompanied a little girl of the OSE to London. Walking through the West End of the city she noticed the Bolivian Consulate and enquired about their office in Paris. She was told that there was no such Consulate there. All consular matters for France and England had to be directed through the London office. The Consul agreed to see her and she told him Kalman's story. To her surprise he opened a drawer, pulled out a visa and said that he had been waiting for eight months for its owner. In his experience, there had never been a renewal of a six-month visa for Bolivia. Niny was prepared to wait for the renewal, but the Consul could do nothing until we obtained the transit visas for Spain, Portugal and Brazil. Geographically, and administratively, the Bolivian visa was the last in the sequence.

Niny, Kalman and I were sent from place to place in the totally disorganised, nerve-wracking atmosphere of post-war Paris. Kalman obtained a boat ticket, but for reasons totally unknown to us, was unable to obtain a Spanish visa and we decided he would take a boat from Bordeaux to Lisbon in order to stay within the time limit. The Consul of London told us on the telephone to send him Kalman's passport and promised to send it back personally by return mail. What a relief! Kalman packed his suitcase, but no letter from London ever arrived. Each time we called London, we were told that the visa would be sent the following day.

Kalman unpacked and said, "I knew it, I'll never see my brothers again." The visa finally arrived on the evening of the boat's departure from Bordeaux. Niny, Kalman and I again engaged in a race against time from Taverny to Paris, Niny at the travel agency, Kalman and myself at the Austerlitz station lining up to buy the ticket for Bordeaux. At last, Kalman jumped onto the last car of a train packed with Portuguese and Spanish immigrants, and was surrounded by luggage and children. The engine whistled, the train started off and Niny arrived just in time to hand the ticket to Kalman. He was the first boy to leave us and we did not even have time to say goodbye.

It took three months before we received a long letter from him written in Yiddish. Moshe read it to us after dinner that evening and everyone listened in total silence. All were candidates for emigration and each was anxious to learn about the details of the experience. Essentially, the letter said, "My two brothers received me very well, but they do not understand me. It is very hot here and everybody wears short sleeves. My brothers show everyone the camp numbers tattooed on my arm. I am an odd creature, a living museum piece. My brothers and I have little in common. I am going to find work, save enough money and then return to Taverny. Write to me quickly to tell me that my place is not taken and will always be reserved for me." Not a word was spoken. Moshe continued reading because there was a postscript. "Niny, I love you. I was afraid to tell you. Please wait for me. When I come back, we will get married."

A roar of laughter eased the unbearable tension created by Kalman's letter. We knew not to answer Kalman's note. In order for Kalman to make a new life, there was no turning back. This was our decision, no matter how heartbreaking, we would not reply to any of the boys' initial letters of distress. As soon as everyone found a place, Taverny would no longer exist.

As it turned out, Kalman worked as a delivery man in Bolivia, practised many trades and finally opened his own business. Within 20 years he became an international businessman in La Paz. During a trip to Paris he went to the OSE and asked for Niny. It took two weeks to find her, but Kalman waited patiently. When he met her he asked "Have you waited for me? I live in La Paz, but once we are married, we will move wherever you want." Niny had already married and was a mother. His love for her endures to this day. He never married and calls from time to time to hear her voice.

Many other boys were found by uncles, aunts or distant cousins who had left central Europe before the war and had moved to the United States, South America, Canada or Australia. The news about the mass murders of Jews by the Nazis had shocked them and they felt guilt for having lived a comparatively carefree life. When they recognised the name of one of their relatives on the lists of survivors, they sought to help. Thus, many of our young people received news from an uncle or aunt, unknown to them in most instances. These letters were written in warm terms and invited the youngsters to join them. They frequently sent money for the journey, along with an affidavit, a document essential to obtain the immigration visa. A ticket usually followed soon after the visa.

We were convinced that all of these persons were probably rich and that Brooklyn, where most of the letters originated, was the Champs Elysées of New York. We did not know that in fact, Brooklyn was one of the poorer sections of New York, with crumbling red brick houses and outside staircases. We also did not know that the uncles, aunts or cousins were factory workers and labourers and that in many cases, the women contributed the travel money required by cleaning houses.

Even though an American visa was not as difficult to obtain as Kalman's, it was still an extremely complicated procedure. The American Consulate located at that time in Place de la Concorde requested not only a passport, but also a certificate of good character and a great number of documents about the emigrant. After a waiting period, the applicant was invited for a final interview.

Meyer-Tzvi

When it was Meyer-Tzvi's turn, I reminded him that he was supposed to be 17 years old and not 21, since it was much easier to obtain a visa for a youngster. We suggested that he shave his beard to look younger, but Meyer-Tzvi explained that several hundred members of his father's former congregation were waiting for him in New York and had prepared a home for him. Since he was going to be that community's rabbi he could not very well arrive beardless. I let him go to the Consulate by himself, even though he understood neither English nor French. On the following day he proudly returned to Taverny with his passport and visa for the United States.

A few weeks before his departure, he showed me a picture of a lovely young girl and told me that she was his fiancée and that he would like us to organise a special dinner party in their honour. I was dumbfounded. Meyer-Tzvi explained to me that the rabbi of a community had to be a married man and that upon his arrival in New York he should at least be engaged. He explained that he heard about this young woman, a distant cousin from his hometown who had survived and was living in a displaced person's camp in Germany. He had written to her and they became engaged. He stated that as soon as she was able to come to the United States, they would get married. On a Saturday evening, after Shabbat, we celebrated his engagement with the young girl's photo pinned to the wall. They had never met. She had to wait two years before getting a visa. They were married immediately upon her arrival and are very happily married.

Unforeseen complications arose many times as in the case of the two boys who had used a friend's train ticket that was reserved strictly for the owner.

They had been caught and a police report had been filed. The boys paid no attention to the incident, but it resulted in a court appearance. Without a clean police record, their departure for the United States was in jeopardy. The only solution was for the Director of the French railroad to withdraw the complaint. Since he was an important official, convincing him was not an easy task, but eventually he complied with my request and the boys were able to obtain a visa for America.

Simon

When Simon was about to leave, he received a letter informing him that his mother had survived in their hometown in Czechoslovakia. He wrote to her and she asked him to come back. It was a very delicate situation for Simon. Of course he wanted to see his mother but he wanted to live in the United States. However, crossing the border with an American visa would jeopardise his return. He decided to contact the Czechoslovakian Consul in Paris, who suggested that he meet his mother at a first class hotel in Prague where they would not be disturbed and he issued to Simon a diplomatic passport.

Prague was decorated with flags and banners and an impressive number of soldiers and policeman surrounded the station. Unaware of the occasion, Simon asked innocently what was happening. A policeman asked him to show his passport and grew suspicious. He found it strange that such a young man was carrying a diplomatic passport and did not know that Marshall Tito, the President of Yugoslavia, was coming on an official visit. He took him to the police station. The authorities were likewise suspicious about his being a diplomat. Simon asked them to call the Consul. It took several hours to reach him, but in the end the Consul vouched for his employee. Simon was released and raced to the hotel where he arrived the same time as Tito. He and his mother did not leave the premises for three days, ignoring the festivities around them. Simon persuaded his mother to follow him to the United States and a few years later she was able to do so. She was a great support to her son's achieving an independent life.

As for the Czechoslovakian Consul in Paris, he was recalled to his country and disappeared. Neither Simon nor anyone else ever heard of him again.

Herschel

Everyone called Herschel "Katsef, the butcher" for he had learned his father's trade and worked at Olida, a meat factory. Katsef had been lucky to find a truly rich uncle in America, a successful businessman. But Katsef had no intentions of changing his way of life. In the evenings he would don a pair of tight worn-out trousers, a coat much too small for him, worn-out shoes and a filthy, shiny cap. He rushed out to take care of our cow. We owned a cow in Taverny, an unexpected consequence of a visit by the Rabbi from Klausenburg, a concentration camp survivor on his way to the United States. He had liked everything about our home except that there was no kosher milk. Kosher milk is simply regular cow's milk, drawn under special supervision to be certain that there is no addition of donkey milk, which is forbidden by Jewish law.

The Rabbi had promised to send money for a cow upon his arrival in New York. We did not think it likely that he would remember, but we were surprised to have delivery of a beautiful black and white, Dutch cow. We put the cow up in the former stables and the boys who had once lived in the country were particularly delighted, fighting for the right to milk the cow and to look after her. Eventually, the butcher assumed full care of the cow, which he named Judith and cared for with great love. Katsef, however, had committed a great sin by eating pork sausage at the meat factory where he worked and went to atone at the nearby yeshiva in Fublaines. He asked me to take care of Judith during his two week absence and reminded me that since it is winter now and the cow cannot go outside, she must have the necessary exercise, so please run her around the park three times each day.

Regretfully, I did not take these instructions very seriously and one evening returning late from Paris, I heard the heartbreaking moans of the cow. I rushed to the telephone to call the vet, while our janitor led the cow out of the stables. She slumped to the ground, never getting up again and the vet could do nothing for her but witness her death. The cow's belly had swollen terribly and the doctor told me that it was from lack of exercise. He told me the cow should have been taken out and that in addition the hay was also too wet. I did not know what I would say to Katsef.

The boys watched silently as we spread a blanket over the cow. After they left for work on the following day, I had the animal removed. While I was waiting for the truck to arrive I heard terrible moaning once again. Crouching next to the cow was the butcher, crying his heart out. He said he had dreamt that the cow had died and jumped onto the first train to make sure that it had only been a dream. To his great distress his premonition was correct.

These events prompted the butcher to accept his uncle's invitation to go to Cincinnati. Because he was sent a first class plane ticket that only rich people could afford at the time, Niny and I decided to buy Herschel proper clothing and a suitcase so that he would not feel awkward on the plane. We stood waiting for him at the Orly terminal in Paris, a luxurious airport where diplomats and their elegant wives strolled up and down the aisles, followed by porters carrying their trunks and leather travel bags. We had been well advised to buy a decent outfit for Herschel! But when he arrived, Herschel was empty handed and dressed in his everyday clothes. Seeing the disappointment on our faces, he explained that his uncle in Cincinnati was definitely rich enough to buy him new clothes and that there was no reason for him to travel in a new outfit. So he had given all of his possessions, including the newly purchased items, to those less fortunate. The stewardess could not believe that he travelled without any luggage and his fellow passengers looked at him with disgust. To my mind, Herschel personified the image of the lonely, wandering Jew who left nothing behind and who had no idea of what the future might bring. Like so many others he wrote to us that his uncle did not understand him and that he was going to leave. He settled in New York where he became a furrier and enjoyed an excellent reputation. He married a young non-Jewish American woman and apparently never talked about his childhood to her or to his two sons. Then one day he jumped out of a window and killed himself.

Eric

One after the other, about 40 of our children left for the United States. The house gradually emptied and the OSE asked us to take children who were in transit, or accept temporary guests with special problems.

The first special problem child who arrived was Eric, who had been born without hands or feet. He was 16 but looked only about six years old. His father, a doctor in Vienna, had applied for visas to America for his entire family when Austria was annexed to Germany in 1938. He received only three visas, for his wife, his daughter who was eight years older than Eric, and for himself. Only people in good health were accepted by America and Eric was refused entry. The parents wanted to cancel their departure but the Consul was adamant that they leave. He assured them that in five years they would be American citizens and could have their son join them.

Unhappy and broken-hearted, Eric's parents left him with his grandmother in Antwerp. On May 10, 1940, the Germans entered neutral Belgium and in the chaos that followed, the exodus to Southern France began. The grandmother left with her grandson and died on the road during a bombardment near Rouen. The little boy was brought to an orphanage and stayed there until the end of the war. In 1945 his parents began their search for him. They found him, paid the orphanage for the years he had spent there and asked the OSE to keep Eric in a children's home until they could obtain a visa for him.

The OSE was convinced that our boys, who had seen just about everything, would have no problems accepting Eric. But for me, it was a shock. Upon my return from a trip to Paris, I saw a little boy perched on a chair, knitting a long red scarf. The knitting needles seemed to move by themselves, firmly tucked into the sleeves of his coat. Large tears ran down his cheeks to his harelip. I had to step out of my office to regain my senses. When I re-entered, he explained in a thin, little voice that he had been waiting for a long time but was afraid to leave the office on his own. I took him to the dining room and the other boys accepted him without discomfort. He had feared this moment of meeting strangers, of perhaps scaring them, but everything went well.

Eric ate very properly, tucking fork, spoon or knife into his sleeve. He would have been lost with short sleeves. He moved very quickly on his stumps and soon became everyone's friend, teaching the boys French and writing letters for them. He resented being treated like a child, after all, he was 16 years old.

During a trip to the American Consulate in Paris, the ticket controller and passengers asked me, "What happened to your little boy?" "Was it an accident or was he born like that?" It became an excruciating train ride for us even though the questions were asked out of concern.

Eric was comfortable with us but remained terrified of strangers and stayed in his room when guests arrived for the Shabbat. We respected his wishes and brought him dinner. After the visitors left, he would come downstairs, relieved and smiling.

Having graduated from school, Eric refused to continue his studies, but I insisted he do so. I was convinced that keeping busy was good for him. I drove him to school on the handlebars of my bicycle and when I picked him up after his first day, he was beaming with joy. No one had asked any questions about his deformities. He had made friends with a black boy, who was as different from the others as himself and he subsequently became the best student of his class.

His parents and now-married sister wrote to him regularly. One day they sent a package containing clothing for a young 16-year-old boy of normal size. We sent a photo of Eric to his parents and used all our tact and skill to break the news of Eric's overall condition to them.

When Eric was ready to embark for the United States, I placed him in the care of a tall, strong boy who was also going there. The letter we received from him convinced us once more that sometimes those perceived to be the weakest possess great strength. Eric's companion wrote, "It was a horrible trip. We travelled on a Liberty Ship (an American freighter that had carried troops and materials to France at the time of the invasion and had been converted to a passenger ship). I was sick throughout the voyage and could not leave my cabin. I was very fortunate to have Eric, who took care of me tirelessly. He was constantly on the go."

We were without any news from Eric for a long time. A letter finally arrived "I wasn't able to write to you sooner because my parents put me into a hospital as soon as I arrived. The doctors made me wear prostheses on my arms and legs. I am very unhappy for I cannot manage with them. I have lost my freedom of movement. I am writing to you in the middle of the night and have secretly removed the devices. I would like to come back." As usual we could not answer his plea and do not know how Eric fared in later life.

France

After Eric's departure, the OSE sent us a rabbi and his large family, originally from Hungary, who were waiting to leave for the United States. In order to escape the Germans, the family had hidden in a forest during the war, moving from one hiding place to another. In addition to his own ten children, the rabbi's sister had given him responsibility for her two boys. He thus had twelve children aged 5-21. When he was unable to trace his nephews' parents after the war, the rabbi married them to his oldest daughters.

The rabbi was a calm and distinguished individual. His wife was very energetic and took care of all their children. I became somewhat impatient over their long stay in our house, especially because the oldest daughter was nine months pregnant. Eventually they moved to Paris. Soon after leaving Taverny, newspapers carried a story of a couple that had clandestinely boarded as passengers on a boat in Le Havre. The man had been discovered and was forced to leave the ship, but the woman could not be found. During the night, cries coming from a covered lifeboat led to the discovery of a young woman who did not speak any French and who was about to give birth. A little girl was born in the infirmary and was named "France" after the name of the ship.

I was overcome with remorse at the idea of the shy young woman giving birth on a ship amongst strangers and I decided to visit her family at their Paris hotel. When I asked her husband as to whether he had been at Le Havre, he replied, "Yes, my wife is still there, they are unable to find her!" I congratulated him, "Mazel Tov! You have a daughter!" I translated for him the article about the circumstances of France's birth and the father was furious. "How dare they give her such a name. She will be called Sara-Rivka, just as we had decided!" Having been born on a French vessel, the little girl was issued a French passport and the nursing mother was permitted to accompany her. That is how a new-born enabled its parents to settle in the United States for the father now had no problems obtaining an American passport.

François

Our last guest was a 17-year-old boy named François, who had lost all of his family in the concentration camps and had been to every single children's home of the OSE, each of which expelled him. To my great surprise, I found him to be a calm, extremely gentle young man with excellent manners. He spoke French very well and I allowed him to take over management of the office, answering the telephone, doing the correspondence and running errands. He was very efficient. I also gave him the cash box containing the boys' pocket money and put him in charge of its distribution. He also administered our monthly budget.

After his departure for the United States, the OSE called to find out how I had managed to keep François, described as an "inveterate kleptomaniac," for such a long time. At first I was furious that they had dared to send a child with that problem to a children's home without informing us. On second thought, had I been warned in advance, I probably would not have entrusted François with the pocket money and the budget. Confidence in him had proven to be the best possible therapy.

The boys who had not been able to find their parents or other family returned to their initial dream, to go to Palestine. The British Government had stopped all permits. Palestine had become a tightly secured fortress and Jews were not admitted.

Weary of waiting in the German camps for a hypothetical international solution, many displaced Jews attempted to breach the British blockade by entering illegally. Travelling under desperate circumstances, sailing in old worn-out crafts, they endangered their lives time and again, often under the cover of night. To counter these illegal efforts, the British Government confined captured immigrants to camps on Cyprus. Many thousands of Jews were once again fenced in behind barbed wire.

Fully aware of the dangers of embarking for Palestine, the young people of Taverny were hesitant to leave. A dozen of them decided to take the risk and started off, either alone or in groups. All but one succeeded and that one was taken to Cyprus.

Another 11 of our children were on board the Exodus when it arrived in Haifa. When the British authorities refused entry, the ship returned to port Port Vendres and from there went to Hamburg. Some found the courage to try again and still others returned to France and settled in Paris.

The last child to remain in Taverny had discovered relatives in Australia but was reluctant to leave. "I have never had a family life, I don't know what it is like. I am much too afraid of being involved in it now." By the end of 1947, everyone had left and the castle of Vaucelles at Taverny was closed down. For Niny and myself it was a very sad moment. We felt miserable, like orphans ourselves.

Niny settled in Paris and I went to Strasbourg. Both of us began to raise families and when we met we did not dare to talk about our boys because we did not know what happened to them. It was too painful. We had severed the ties, why revive the memories? We were convinced that we would never again see or hear from the children of Ambloy and Taverny.

8

LIFE JOURNEYS —
20 YEARS LATER IN NEW YORK

*T*herefore, in the Spring of 1965, Niny and I were very surprised and happy to receive invitations to a dinner being held in New York to commemorate the 20th anniversary of the liberation of Buchenwald. The invitation was signed by the "Committee of the Buchenwald-Taverny Group."

A cable followed: "Come, you are our guest. Cable date of your arrival." Niny was unable to attend, so I travelled alone. During the flight I closely studied a large photo of the Ambloy group. Twenty years had passed and I feared that I would not recognise them.

They stood waiting behind the large glass front at Kennedy Airport, holding bouquets of flowers and the very same photo of Ambloy. They also mistrusted their memories. A wave of emotion swept over us as we greeted each other. It was obvious that the intervening years had not dampened the affection between us.

Throughout that evening, the former members of Taverny arrived from different parts of the United States. Many of them had not seen each other since Taverny. They used their former nicknames, such as "Redhead" but in the meantime the redhead had gone bald. Unable to comprehend the depths of our emotions, the wives remained reserved.

Among the members of the Committee presiding over the dinner party were Leo Margulies and Moshe, The Rabbi, now with a long grey beard. Moshe rose and offered the blessing: "Blessed art thou, Oh Lord our G-D, King of the universe, who has kept us in life, and hast preserved us, and enabled us to reach this season." Everyone rose to their feet and ardently and passionately repeated the words. He then continued: "We have not gathered today to glory in being alive, but to remember those who are dead. Tonight's gathering serves as a continuation of the Yom Kippur in Ambloy when some had refused to participate in the Yizkor service, refused because there was still hope. Today, we know that our parents and our relatives will never return. We have been struggling for 20 years to succeed in our new lives. They have been difficult years during which we had neither the time nor the peace of mind to mourn our parents, our brothers and sisters, our families and the cities and villages from which we came. The time has come now when we can do so. Let us rise and think of them, let us say Kaddish — the prayer for the dead." Everyone recited the Kaddish aloud together, and wept.

After a long silence, Moshe continued in his strong voice: "We are the remains of Ezekiel, having recovered our breath. We are the dead whom God has resurrected. Let us celebrate. For Passover, we have unleavened bread, for Chanukah we light eight candles, for the Succot feast of tabernacles, we have the Succah. And here is what I have found for our celebration." He held up a cracked bowl filled with potatoes. "None of you have forgotten how much potatoes meant to us in Buchenwald, raw or cooked, peeled or unpeeled. The peelings alone were a treasured possession." He continued his speech, mixing tears with laughter and despair with hope. He was their old Moshe, the leader they remembered.

The dinner progressed in an affectionate, warm and intimate atmosphere. Leo Margulies spoke of the common past that had created such a strong bond between the survivors of Buchenwald. The purpose of Taverny had been fulfilled. It had created a home and substitute family with strong and lasting ties.

Then I was asked to speak.

I conveyed regards from Niny and then explained the reasons for our silence, for not replying to their letters in the beginning. I then addressed the wives who must have felt overlooked and overwhelmed: "It is thanks to you, that your husbands have achieved a degree of happiness and contentment. It is you who helped them to find their equilibrium." Afterwards, they told me that they were deeply touched and reassured by these words.

I was given a bracelet as a present: "To Judith — to remember the 20th anniversary — from the boys of Buchenwald and Taverny." But I received much more than this. They now offered also the gift of sharing their stories. They had wanted to see me, to present their families to me, and to start talking about their pasts, many of them for the first time in their lives. In Taverny, we had never asked many questions, the past was still much too painful. But 20 years later in New York, I wanted to ask about their parents and families, about their education and upbringing. Had the camps affected their behaviour and the choices they made? How had they raised their children? How did they view their lives?

Most of the children of Buchenwald who now lived in the United States seemed to have integrated into American life while preserving strong connections to traditional Jewish family and community life.

Their reluctance to speak about the Camps to relatives and to interested strangers was dictated by a need for self-preservation. They had been hurt so deeply and so humiliated that they avoided arousing pity, which was perceived also as a kind of humiliation. They sought to control their anger through hard work and success, which also lessened guilt over having survived when so many did not. They did not want to waste the gift of life.

They kept their nightmares to themselves, for they knew that only those who had lived through the camps could understand.

My former boys of Taverny refused me only one thing, to take me to a newly opened bar on the 66th floor of a skyscraper. Sixty-six was the barracks number in Buchenwald where most of them had been imprisoned together and which reminded them of their indescribable sufferings.

They responded openly to my questions, some briefly, others at length. I have written down the accounts as they were related to me but with anonymity for the speaker and minor editing for flow of language.

David — The Businessman

David was 19 years old upon his arrival in Ambloy. He came with a violin from Weimar, the one he refused to surrender upon leaving Buchenwald. He had decided to become a dental technician while in France and was now living with his wife and three children in a large house in a wealthy suburb of New York where he told me his story.

I was born in Czechoslovakia in 1929. There were six children in our family, three girls and three boys. Shortly before the war, my father had sent my older sister to New York. I was deported first to Auschwitz with my older brother Abraham, then to other camps where I frequently met up with my cousin Moshe, the Rabbi. The three of us were together in Buchenwald when it was liberated. When the SS ordered us to leave the camp, Moshe advised us to disobey. As it turned out, had we stepped through the gate when we were kicked out by the Germans, we would have been shot.

Near the gate I decided to play dead and let myself fall near the dead bodies lying by the side of the road. An SS soldier struck me hard on the head, but despite the pain, I did not move. There followed a terrible confusion mingled with blows and screams and suddenly there was dead silence. I waited about 30 minutes before I opened my eyes and lifted my head. I saw a huge tank with black American soldiers who were chewing gum. I thought this must be the secret weapon of the Americans, some super-intelligent, cud-chewing animal. Then I passed out.

I had typhus and a Czechoslovakian doctor saved my life. When I was finally allowed to leave the infirmary, Moshe stole chickens because Jewish mothers had always taught us that chicken soup was a cure for everything. I gave my sister's address in the United States to an American soldier and asked him to tell her that Abraham and I were alive. He delivered the message.

Fifteen years later, that soldier stepped into my New York office to visit and we recognised each other immediately.

From Buchenwald we went to France, then to New York on visas and affidavits provided by my uncle.

When I asked David what he remembered about the children's homes he had been in, he told me the following:

I have only general memories of Ambloy and Taverny. The same goes for the Camps — I have completely forgotten the details. We were handed everything at Taverny; all problems were kept from us. We thought that we were entitled to everything because we had survived. In a way we lived removed from reality. It was too good.

When we arrived in the United States, we thought we would be entering a paradise with angels to shelter us. Reality was different and we should have been better prepared for it. I suffered a terrible depression during the first week. My uncle knew what had happened in the Camps. As for me, I quickly realised that talking of the past would make me an outsider. The people here said for us to forget about the past and get on with your life.

All of us set out to ask for work in all kinds of factories. I did not yet understand a word of English and all day saw people refusing us by shaking their heads. I felt like a calf being led to market to be sold, but not saleable.

One evening, while walking home to my older sister's apartment where I lived with Abraham, I noted the factory on the first floor that made electric watches for sports events. During a conversation in German with the owner, I was hired to look after the workshop during his absences and later he taught me how to perforate and cut pieces of metal according to a pattern. That was my first job.

I had enormous problems adjusting to the American way of life. American culture seemed based entirely on material values and appeared extremely shallow. After two years in the United States, I still did not speak English well. I had been torn from comfortable surroundings, where I had felt at home and was thrown into a society where I was nothing. I was 21 years old, but not able to function. I finally took evening courses in English and received a high school diploma. By 1949 I did not feel as lost any more — I could at least speak and understand the language — and I started going places with my cousin Fanny, who was born in this country. She helped me to understand the United States and later she became my wife.

I started to work for myself, bought several drugstores and began to invest in real estate. I became wealthy.

My manner was greatly influenced by my past. When I was deported at age 18, I had no idea what it meant to resist or risk your own life. When I saw the television movie, "Holocaust," I felt ashamed of myself and of those supposedly intelligent and determined persons who were not aware that one had to show physical courage to survive and had to offer one's life to resist the enemy. Ignorant of this fact, I and thousands of others had been trapped, unable to show the slightest resistance. The Warsaw Ghetto fighters are heroic, for not only did they fight the enemy, but they fought their rabbi's teachings. God works miracles only if we contribute. I am ashamed of the doctrines of our religion that emphasise passivity and that regard suffering simply as a punishment from God.

Since I was the first-born, my father sent me to a yeshiva and I was still very observant upon my arrival in the United States. But I have gradually abandoned living by commandments.

When my children were very young I went to see my cousin Moshe to tell him that I did not intend to raise them as my father had raised me. Being the eldest, I had been expected to be the most knowledgeable and the most pious of all. Moshe told me that I would regret this decision. And he was right. Although I wanted to raise my children in the Jewish tradition, I decided to free them from the obligation to excel. Today, I know that my attitude has kept them from fully developing their capacities and my children lack ambition. I should have taught them to realise the importance of their particular mission. Had I the opportunity to do it over, I would have preferred living a religious Jewish life in Jerusalem.

I asked David how he felt about the Germans.

> Asking for compensation from the Germans has been a great ordeal. Nothing can ever be done to redeem the sufferings in the Camps. To this day I curse them and wish all those responsible to die. And yet, I do not hate all Germans — I hate their philosophy. Hitler was not an accident of nature. He was the product of the philosophy of Nietzsche, Kant and Hegel who glorified the superman, the superior creature. Hitler served as an instrument of this German mentality that eventually sought out the feeble and unproductive persons to be killed. Then they turned to murdering Jews.
>
> During a group trip through Europe a few years ago, I had to pass through Germany. I was amazed. In my mind, all Germans looked like the SS soldiers in the Camps, tall, erect, dressed in black, true supermen. I was shocked that the customs officers that checked our passport at the border were short and fat and one was carrying a small purse. I asked myself how these 'supermen' had managed to intimidate and terrorise us in the camps. I was enraged to realise that they had the strength to impose their superiority on me. I felt ashamed by what they had done to my mind.
>
> During my two-day stay in Germany I closely observed each and every man, thinking 'could this one have been a guard?' The Germans however, sang and drank beer and were totally oblivious and without remorse. To think that some self-proclaimed historians dare say that the Camps never existed!

Moshe — The Rabbi

In the Camps and later in Taverny, Moshe had been a leader. Moshe became an Orthodox rabbi, who abides by the traditional texts yet is open to modern scientific thought. He is renowned throughout the Jewish world for his books of responsa which offer the religious Jew solutions to problems created by modern life. He gave me the following account of his past.

I was born in Hungary in 1925. My father was head of a yeshiva and a kollel, a yeshiva for adults. Of the six children in our family, I was the fifth. I went to a Hungarian school for two years and then to heder and then the yeshiva. My father had connections with the outside world and realised what was about to happen. He succeeded in getting me a visa for the Holy Land in 1942 but it was already too late. When we were deported in 1944, my father had no illusions. He was convinced that he would die and used the water distributed by the Germans to wash his hands and recite the prayer for the dead.

I was completely alone when I arrived in Auschwitz. I refuse to talk about this period. I never mention it to my children and I still have nightmares every night.

Thanks to an affidavit granted by an uncle in New York, I was able to leave for the United States in 1947. I was very unhappy there because my uncle was not a religious man. I left after only two days. I found the address of the Rabbi of Klausenburg who had visited us in Taverny and was very well received by him. Eighteen months later I was head of one of his yeshivoth and soon opened my own school. In the beginning it was small and poor, but now it occupies several buildings. I have a tremendous influence on my pupils. After getting married, they frequently settle in this neighbourhood and become members of my congregation. I have also opened a kindergarten and intend to set up a heder and a school.

The upsurge of religious life in the United States is a consequence of the aftermath of the Holocaust. Before the war there were 800 pupils in the yeshivoth, now there are 50,000. I am very proud to have participated in this development. My own children are raised as I was raised by my father. But I am even stricter with them than he was with me. I allow no

Elie Wiesel with Moshe the Rabbi (Menashe Klein), Jerusalem, April 1986

concessions. Having been deported taught me that you could only rely on yourself. I believe that in writing this book you have undertaken a very important task. Auschwitz must never be forgotten.

Moshe has remained close friends with Isaiah, a Polish Jewish boy who had gone from Taverny to Jerusalem to live near his rabbi from Gur. For a Hungarian Jew to mingle with a Chasidic follower of a Polish rabbi would have been unthinkable before the war.

Isaiah had shown Moshe's books of responsa to the Rabbi of Gur. He was extremely impressed by the books and its author. He proposed a marriage between his own nephew and Moshe's eldest daughter with hopes of creating a dynasty. The two young people met, liked each other and were later married.

This union had great symbolic meaning for the Rabbi of Gur because it represented reconciliation with Hungarian Judaism, and all these events unfolded from Isaiah and Moshe's friendship at Taverny.

One day, large posters from New York covered walls of houses in North Jerusalem where Moshe was going to lay the cornerstone for a new religious quarter. All Chasidic rabbis of note had come. I went to see him also. Moshe, in his discourse, evoked memories of his hometown and the Jews who had lived there, most of whom had been murdered. His objective was to bring this community back to life in the Holy Land, the cradle of Jewish religious life and its origins. At the end of his speech, Moshe turned to me and said, "I hope I did not disappoint you." I was deeply moved.

Raphael: The Independent

Raphael was the young man who, in his despair, left his room at Taverny only at night to listen to the wind. In New York I learned about the wonderful memories he had kept of his childhood in Rumania. He talked openly about his sweet and affectionate mother and about Auschwitz.

> At the time of my arrival in Auschwitz I was only 15 years old, but already nearly six feet tall. On the first day there, the Germans forced six men to carry a rail, the two tallest men at either end. The smaller men in the middle lifted their shoulders a little, pretending to help, but the weight of the load remained on the two tallest. I was in the front at first and at the back when we returned but the weight was the same. All I could see was my comrades' backs. The weight was so great, the effort so terrible, that it caused me to cry. That evening in the barracks, I saw that the other boy, even taller than I, was also crying. It was Moshe and from that day on we remained together, sharing everything.
>
> He saved my life twice.
>
> The first time was in Buchenwald a few days before the arrival of the Americans. A Ukrainian guard hit me so hard on

the head that it left me temporarily paralysed. I remained sprawled on my cot for several days until hunger drove me out. An SS soldier yelled at me and wanted to know what I was doing. Moshe just happened to come by. Any other prisoner would have continued on his way, but Moshe stopped and spoke to the SS soldier. He told him to leave me alone, that he knew me and that I was not normal, crazy. The SS turned away and I was able to return to the barracks.

The second time he saved my life was after liberation. I had overeaten and was deathly sick with diarrhoea. Moshe nursed me tirelessly for three weeks. He burned bread and gave it to me as a kind of coal to absorb fluids. I would have died without him. I know that he doesn't need anything, but I wish I could do something for him to express my gratitude.

I also contracted typhus in Buchenwald. Again it was Moshe who placed my name on the list of people leaving for France. When it was time to go, he simply came to the hospital and carried me in his arms to the train. Once, during our stay in Écouis, we were taken on a sightseeing tour of Paris and visited the Eiffel Tower. The elevator was broken and Meyer-Tzvi, still suffering from frostbite, could barely walk. I did what Moshe had done for me and I carried Meyer-Tzvi in my arms. But by the time we had reached the first level the other boys were already returning, so I quietly turned around to follow them so as not to get lost.

In Taverny, I learned my father's trade, printing. I managed to trace my older sister to Sweden, but I was unable to obtain a visa to join her. I tried to go to Israel on the Exodus, but only eleven places were available and I was the twelfth applicant. When Taverny was closed down, two other boys and I went to a yeshiva near Paris. The members of this school were preparing to leave for the United States and after their departure the three of us had nowhere to go. We soon found another group called the "Wise Men of Lublin" who obtained visas for the United

States for us. But their yeshiva in New York did not accept me because I did not have the money to pay for room and board. Once more I had nowhere to go. Finally, Meyer-Tzvi put me up in the large house belonging to an unmarried uncle of his. I was given the opportunity to study at the yeshiva run by the Rabbi of Klausenburg.

I felt terribly lonely until I was reunited with Tibor and Yossi, my comrades from Taverny. Every morning I used to pray in a little synagogue near Meyer-Tzvi's house where a man who noticed me there said he wouldn't mind having me as a son-in-law. I was only 19 years old and had no desire to marry. So I changed synagogues until I heard that the young girl was safely wed. However, this man was persistent and proposed that I marry his niece Miriam. One morning, Meyer-Tzvi's uncle said that a young girl had come to visit and he wanted me to meet her. My friends told me I had nothing to lose and so I complied with the uncle's wish. I chatted with Miriam until 2 o'clock in the morning and a month later we were engaged. I delayed our wedding because I had no job and it took me a year to find one. In the meantime, Miriam's uncle taught me how to engrave tombstones for his shop, but I received no pay for six months. Finally, I started off working at $20.00 a week and after my marriage, was paid the considerable weekly sum of $30.00. The other boys who had been at Taverny — all 40 of them — came to my wedding.

We have a girl and three boys and I am a very strict father. I want them to be devout and insist that they all learn a trade. I make sure that they know that I despise abusive language, be it in English or in Yiddish. And I never talk about the Camps. My wife cannot understand why not, but my youngest son does. He was once hit by a car and had to remain in the hospital for a long time. He told me that his pain had been so severe that he could not talk about it.

Raphael told me that he felt at home in Brooklyn and that he respected the United States because the basic interests of Americans were the same as his own. He too wanted to be independent.

Herself an American, Miriam provided the security he needed without pushing him into the competitive American way of life which he avoided. She also understood the importance of his ties with the past and kept her home always open for his friends. Raphael has left Brooklyn only once and that was to travel to Switzerland for his sister's wedding.

Meyer-Tzvi — The Penitent

We celebrated Meyer-Tzvi's engagement to an unknown cousin before he left Taverny for New York. He was only 19 and yet an entire New York community awaited his arrival for he was the heir to a rabbinic dynasty.

A slim and pleasant woman opened the door to their Brooklyn apartment. Rabbi Meyer-Tzvi was seated at a long table covered with white linen. He was an impressive figure with a long beard and heavy glasses, dressed in the traditional outfit of pumps, stockings and black pants, a long caftan and a round broad rimmed hat. I listened to Meyer-Tzvi's account over cakes and tea that his wife had prepared.

> I was born in Hungary in 1925, the eldest of seven children. My father was a well-known rabbi. For two years I lived in a ghetto where I worked very hard. My mother and the six younger children were deported long before I was. I was 18 years old when my father and I were taken to Auschwitz. The convoy transported 3,500 women and men and only 350 were declared fit for work, fit to live a little longer. When we arrived in Buchenwald my father was 40 years old and sensed that we would soon be separated for good. He told me not to change my way of dressing, to wear pumps and black socks during the week and white socks during Shabbat. I interpreted his instructions to mean that I must respect every single detail of our way of life, of our traditions. Older inmates of Auschwitz

asked newly arrived prisoners about what they intended to eat since nothing was kosher. Some answered they would eat only soup and others said they would eat everything. I told them that I would decide on a day to day basis. A long time inmate commented that probably I would likely only eat bread and he was right.

By the time I arrived at Buchenwald, I was totally starved and my toes were frozen. At liberation, because of my persistence in eating bread only, I escaped death caused from over-eating. I registered to go to France for I was afraid to return to Hungary because of the Russians. I fought hard to obtain kosher food at Écouis which brought us to Ambloy where Moshe and I lived a Jewish life.

I was convinced that my younger brother would survive, as he was not only a Talmudic genius, but tall and strong. But he died two weeks before liberation. Therefore I had no one left in the world except for three relatives, an uncle in America and, in Germany, an aunt with her daughter whom I later married. The other members of my family did not return from the Camps. My unmarried uncle received me in his house and we still live there. I never went anywhere else.

I am very happy in Brooklyn. Jewish life here completely satisfies me. My children were named after my dead parents, brothers and sisters. Because they were born in this country they consider themselves Americans, even though only my daughters speak English. I taught my sons the Talmud and mathematics. I want them to have the same Jewish education that I received.

After my arrival in New York I continued studying the Talmud, mathematics and astronomy on my own. I calculated the beginning and end of Shabbat in other places when members of my congregation went on trips. This requires very complicated calculations and they have become routine work for me now and yet doing it still makes me nervous. I may be stronger in spirit than when I was young, but my nerves are not.

I am my father's heir. I am in charge of a large community with members who pray in my synagogue and who are my students. Because I am extremely well known, I cannot leave the house without being recognised, so I stay home and feel very isolated. It is always a great pleasure when the former boys of Taverny come to see me.

I never talk about the past to my children, they are not interested. I have, however, written down my memories, first by hand and then typed them in 1964. I would not go through such an ordeal again. I wrote the account of our deportation for my children beginning with Passover in 1944, an ill-fated period for the Jewish people who had to endure such hardship and pain. I was a witness to the terrible catastrophe that engulfed one third of them, yet I refuse to judge God's will. The Jewish people were punished for their sins. Their biggest crime had been to believe that they were on the path of redemption. I went to great pains to write of my sufferings in order to have my children understand that sinners have to accept the wrath of God. They have to be convinced that the holy law and the strict observance of its commandments were the only way to bring about their redemption. We must learn a lesson from the persecutions and sufferings endured in the Camps. We must pray even more fervently and never stray from our traditions. I am very strict with my children. I want all of them to marry someone who has the same convictions and I want them to dedicate their lives to the study of the Talmud.

When I returned to New York in 1980, all of Meyer-Tzvi's children had married and studied according to their father's wishes. He had honoured his father's demand in Auschwitz that he not stray from the path.

Simon — The Worker

For Simon, the lessons learned from his past can be summed up as follows: If you are determined to survive, you will! As a result, he is often judgmental of his comrades, but is not consistent in his views. It should be noted that his son wanted very much to be a part of the conversation. He had attempted to learn what his father had endured by visiting Dachau on his own. On this day he heard the entire account.

I was born in Czechoslovakia in 1927. For us, war began with the German invasion in 1939. Things changed immediately at school. A different mentality ruled.

I was the third of four children. We spoke several languages, including Hungarian, Czechoslovakian and Russian. My father was wealthy. He owned a grocery store and a transportation business, which had carriages and six or seven horses. Although my father was a very religious man, he kept his beard short. He was a Hassidic follower of a relatively non-sectarian rabbi. I went to public school in the mornings, and to heder in the afternoons. Our father taught us to love work, that no task was too menial. To him work was sacred and during summer vacations we had to work in the fields.

One day, when I was 13, my father fell sick. My brother was in the army so I had to distribute the assignments to the drivers. When they returned in the evening, I invited them to a nearby bar for a beer. My mother found out that I had associated with non-Jews and angrily reprimanded me. I asked her what was wrong in inviting your own workmen for a drink. I argued they might have ignored me as too young or taken advantage of the situation and cheated us. Instead they had done an honest day's work which deserved reward.

I had trusted my own judgment and everything had gone well. Using my judgment is what helped to save my life in the Camps. Those who did not survive did not necessarily die of hunger, but often because they gave up. My older brother was like that. He had given up all hope and I kept telling him to be patient, that sooner or later it will be over. I urged him to struggle one day at a time. During the long march after the evacuation of Auschwitz, the Germans shouted that anyone too tired to continue should get on the trucks. Before I could stop him, my brother had gone. I never saw him again. The date was January 22, 1945.

Yes, in the Camps one had to be determined to survive and not believe in miracles. One had to be constantly alert, and hard-working. For a while, I was in a small camp near Auschwitz and worked in a metal factory. The head of our barracks remained behind to clean up the quarters with only a broom at his disposal. I made him a metal shovel at the factory and he was so grateful that he frequently slipped me extra food.

Upon my arrival in Buchenwald, I was taken to the infirmary to be treated for frostbite of my toes. When I started to feel better, I immediately asked whether I could help. I did not want to be expendable. Working allowed me to stay even after I was healed and kept me from starving to death during the last days before liberation. When the infirmary was shut down, I went to Barracks 66. I almost died of overeating after liberation and was near death for one week. I gave not a second thought to returning home. Even the Russians were reluctant to return to their country. My motto became never to look back, to make a new start and to keep looking ahead. I was very happy in France. We were treated as well as the French prisoners of war released from German prison camps. We were handed the same repatriation cards, had the same access to the metro and the trains, and received the same clothing.

The Czechoslovakian consul who came to Écouis needed help to register Czech citizens and I volunteered. Later I accompanied him to Paris and then he sent me to the Hotel de la Reine d'Angleterre in Biarritz where families of embassy employees lived. I remained there for two weeks, but there were no Jews there and I wanted to return to my friends. So I went back to Écouis and then to Ambloy. I began to write my memoirs in Yiddish but gave up. I learned to be an electrician at the ORT.

In the meantime I had located an uncle in America who sent me an affidavit. I thought that he owned a button factory in New York, but he was actually a labourer in a belt factory. I vowed that within ten years I would be independent and rich. At first I lived with my uncle in Brooklyn. He was a religious man and I was no longer observant. On the first Rosh Hashana at synagogue, my neighbour suddenly leaned over and invited me to go to the movies as neither of us was praying. We left and from that day we were inseparable. He was also a Camp survivor.

A month later, he and I found a small apartment in Brighton Beach near New York. We took any work available and were always able to manage. I adjusted my lifestyle according to my income and I never again felt poor. I worked at hotels during the summers, earning as much as $10,000 a season. This allowed me to attend school full time. I completed Grades 9-12 in one and a half years and graduated.

My friend and I became salesmen in a large fabric store. We specialised in curtain making and one day decided to open our own curtain factory. We offered estimates to hotel and office construction sites that had huge bay windows. I was in charge of administration. My partner cut the curtains and my mother, who had arrived two years after we started the business, sewed the material until we were able to afford seamstresses. We didn't feel it worth working ourselves to death. That we had already done in the Camps. Therefore, we worked only five days a week and took long summer and winter vacations. After all, money is only worth what you do with it. When you have a lot, you may lose it all anyway. Look what happened to my father. We eventually accepted a third partner, Marc, a former resident of Taverny, and today we are one big family. When one of us goes away, the others take care of his children.

I remember with great excitement my naturalisation ceremony. All newly arrived immigrants in New York for five years were present at what seemed almost a religious ritual. The judge presiding at the ceremony had himself been an immigrant. He pronounced us as equal full-fledged citizens of the United States. I consider myself totally an American, but all my friends are Jews. Ten percent of my income is distributed to the poor, of which 90% goes to Jewish charities and 10% to non-Jewish welfare organisations, which assist starving children in Biafra or Cambodia. I am terribly upset whenever I hear of hungry children, no matter what their race or religion.

When I filled out the forms for German compensation payments, I was to be examined by a German psychiatrist. When he requested that I describe life in Auschwitz I answered very calmly that every morning, the SS served us freshly squeezed orange juice for breakfast. He became furious and yelled at me in a rage. I yelled back and took off. He knew perfectly well what had happened in Auschwitz.

Naturally I wasn't granted any compensation, but I don't regret my anger. I have gradually overcome my hatred for Germans. It took some time to realise that not all of them are the same, especially those who were born during or after the war. It is not fair to generalise. But I still never buy German products. Nor do my children. I have never set foot on German soil. In fact, I am reluctant to leave the United States.

I have been to Israel though, and was shocked at the lack of Jewish culture among Israelis. A Jew must be aware of the laws even if not living a religious life. My three sons were raised according to these principles. I sent them to Jewish schools because I wanted them to understand Judaism and to feel at ease with religious Jews like my uncle and my mother. As adults they were free to choose their own path entirely.

As far as I am concerned, I do not believe in God. If he really exists, he should be repudiated and charged in a court of law. And still, I continue to go to the synagogue every Friday. I remain an active member of the Jewish community. Once a year, I make a speech for fund raising purposes. I do not find it an easy task, but we raise twice as much money when I am the speaker. I usually ask the congregation what good their money is when my father, who had a lot of money, lost it overnight to the Germans. I remind them they were spared only because they happened to live here. Had they been in Europe like their fellow Jews, they too would have suffered our fate. My speech usually brings tears and doubles the commitment.

Simon's son, present during our entire conversation, told me later how he had resented his father's strict upbringing. Forced to attend synagogue twice a month on Friday evenings, he spent his time chatting with friends, just like his father used to do. Although he disliked the religious studies he is now glad he went because of his comfort with Orthodox Jews.

He was recently engaged to a religious girl and they plan to keep a kosher home.

Marc — The Poster Boy

At the time Marc arrived at Taverny, he was small and his growth appeared stunted. Nearly 30 years later, he was tall, slim and distinguished-looking. He speaks non-accented English and, although more reserved than his friend and partner Simon, he agreed to speak to me.

I was born in Hungary in 1929. I was the only member of my family in the camp. I would not have wanted to be with a father or brother and have to share our rations of bread or soup. I worked in a coal mine. I only survived because I watched my physical hygiene.

In Taverny, I received an affidavit and a ticket from an aunt in New York. When I arrived at her home, she told me that two of my brothers were still alive in Italy. Had I known about this before, I would certainly have joined them. Because she was childless, my aunt had kept the information from me.

I was very unhappy. I immediately found work in a tie factory, but I was 16 years old and found work very boring.

One year later, I signed up for the U.S. army. I had the tattoos removed from my arm and took an Americanised name. I felt more at ease, knew where I belonged, and I started to grow again. I was the youngest officer in the United States and they chose my photo for the recruitment posters of the U.S. army stating "We Want You!"

I stayed in the army for four years and received letters from an American woman who was a friend of Simon's wife. After four years of correspondence, we met, became engaged and were married soon after. My wife did not want me to sign up for another six years in Oklahoma, so Simon employed me. I became a salesman for him and we later became partners. I travel a lot. Right now, I go on business trips to Saudi Arabia and Third World countries. We obtain large orders from those countries.

I never tell anyone that I am Jewish and that I have been in the camps. It serves no purpose and I don't want people to feel sorry for me. When I travel with my children to Israel, I do take them to Yad Vashem, the Museum of the Holocaust. It is the best of its kind.

Not a day goes by that I don't think of the camps. I have learned three basic lessons: First of all, to know people and myself better, to detest for all time the Germans — we never buy any German products; and finally in camp I vowed never to be caught again.

At the moment of liberation I felt sure that nothing of the sort could ever happen again. Now I am not so sure anymore. I went to see my brothers in Israel in 1973. Both are career officers. I went with them to Nablus. They lent me a gun. I had mixed feelings of pride and shame at the same time. In my opinion, the Arabs should have some territory. In any case, Israel won't be able to keep it all.

Eugene — The Taxi Driver

In Taverny, Eugene had been the life and soul of the home and he proudly identified himself playing the accordion in the photos I had brought to New York. He told me that as a taxi driver, he was prepared to talk only in his car. With eyes firmly on the road, during the special "$200 tour," he offered his life story. Born in Hungary of rich parents, he was deported to Yavichewitz, where he was forced to work in the coal mines. By liberation he was in the infamous Barracks 66 of Buchenwald:

> The barracks were divided in two sections, on one side were the Poles protected by Gustav, the head of the block, on the other side were the Hungarians and Rumanians, those he unscrupulously sent to their deaths when young people were requested. I found my brother in Buchenwald after the liberation. He wanted to return home but I didn't out of fear of the communists. He left me behind feeling no remorse even though I was 14 years old at the time, one year younger. I will never forgive him. I hate him and never want to see him again. He sold all of our family belongings and kept all the money for himself. He later went to Israel and only wrote to me when he was short of money. Now he lives in Munich and is very rich. The other day he called me from there just to brag about having the money to make long distance calls. I told him that I never wanted to hear from him again.
>
> We behaved like maniacs when we arrived at Écouis. I think that the religious ones, especially Moshe, really had nerve to demand kosher food. Running through the countryside all day I saw poor French peasants with nothing to eat, while we were

well fed. It was disgusting to hear the religious ones ask for kosher meat and special consideration. When the religious group left for Ambloy I did not want to go along and went to several Buchenwald homes in Paris. But they were chaotic and there was absolutely no discipline. I did not like them at all.

One day I met Gabor, a Hungarian I knew from Écouis, who asked me to come with him to Taverny. He told me it was nice there and so I went. I felt at home right away even though I wasn't observant. Because of you, the home was well run and disciplined and everyone was kept busy.

I really liked it in France. As you can see, I speak perfect French. I used to have a great time in Paris, but perhaps you did not know. I had a girlfriend there who went back to her family in England. So when I obtained an affidavit and an American visa in 1948, I decided to try my luck in the New World. I didn't think that money was lying in the streets of New York, but I felt life would be easier there than it was in France.

The poorest of my three aunts was the most helpful — she cooked my favourite dishes — but the other two were constantly afraid I would ask them for money. I got the message and never set foot again in the homes of the rich aunts and I was too embarrassed to go to the poor one too often. I regretted having left France. I had worked the black market and had enough money.

I finally found a job with a German-Jewish butcher. He was a great old man who treated me like a son. I worked six days a week from early morning until late at night. He paid poorly, but he was extremely good to me personally. I stayed with him for 22 years until he died. His son took over the business but I didn't want to work for him because he bossed me around.

After that I bought a taxi and licence. I was too busy to go to evening classes, so I ended up learning English from the other taxi drivers. I am on my own. I don't want to work for a company. We independent cab owners help one another. I have an intense dislike for the others — the drivers of white roofed cars. I work mostly in the afternoons and evenings and sleep until 11:00 in the morning. I have rented a lovely apartment in the Bronx. I often see Meyer, Daniel's younger brother.

I try not to think of the camps, I want to forget. Why talk about it? I frequently carry German tourists. They are very proper and kind and give large tips. I explain the sights of New York to them in German. When they ask me where I learned their language, I tell them that I was a "Kriegsgefangener" (prisoner of war). I don't blame them — they just obeyed orders. But I really came to hate the Hungarians during the war. The Arrow Cross (Hungarian Nazis) would kill any Jew they came across. They did it out of sheer hatred. I can practically smell their presence and I refuse to carry them in my cab.

The other day while buying a takeout meal in a Jewish restaurant, I noticed that the owner's tattoo number was very close to mine. I asked Leon whether that reminded him of something. I told him who I was and asked if he remembered. He almost fainted. I was correct, we were together in the mines and in the barracks. He served me a triple portion and I said to him that now I didn't need so much, but I could have used it in Yavichewitz! I go back to that restaurant every week and we visit and chat.

Eugene invited me to a Jewish restaurant for lunch. Despite his outward cockiness, he seemed very shy and lonely. He was only 13 when he arrived at camp. He remembered his parents well. His personality and character were just starting to develop but he had to adjust quickly to concentration camp life and recognise the importance of being resourceful. So he acted like an adult then, but when life returned to normal, he lost his self assurance and his social standing crumbled. He has since become a shy, insecure and unhappy man who feels left out and was unable to find someone to marry. He currently has a friend who is a widow whom he pampers and spoils and hopes will one day agree to marry him.

Meyer — The Indecisive

Meyer took care of his older brother Daniel in camp and in Taverny. Meyer explained that Daniel reflected but "I acted". Daniel used to say that they would not make it. Meyer was always alert. He was always there when something was handed out and he learned to survive in the camp.

When I saw him again, Meyer was 49 years old, shy and indecisive. He said that the only time he thinks about the camp is when others talk about it.

> When I hear of those times, memories return to me and I have trouble sleeping. I become restless and nervous. I only watched part of the movie 'Holocaust' because the movie was not realistic. I was there and it was not faithful to the truth. I am sure that no one would have watched it if they had portrayed what really happened there and shown the masses of corpses. As far removed from reality as it was, it still had a tremendous impact on non-Jews. On the days it appeared on television, my barber closed his shop early, so that he would not miss it.
>
> I was 14 years old at the time of liberation. I was very small and did not really understand what was happening. For me, liberation meant that there was suddenly bread to eat. I went to Weimar and stole a bicycle. It was the first bicycle in Buchenwald and I watched it constantly. I once needed to fill the tires and asked a Ukrainian for his pump. In return he wanted me to let him take a short ride. He never came back.
>
> My memories of Taverny are vague, but I was grateful to France and the OSE for having offered a home to the children of Buchenwald.
>
> Those who were not able to leave the camps at that moment and stayed in Germany started dealing in the black market. Some continued this kind of life afterwards because they did not have the chance to slowly re-adjust through living in a children's home and receiving an education like we did.
>
> In New York I lived in the home of a very poor aunt and held

several jobs. At the same time I studied, first at the yeshiva and then at the university. I managed to rent a small apartment and attend evening classes, passing all elementary and high school grades, then going onto a school for electric engineering.

After completing school I was hired by a manufacturer of measurement instruments and I still work for that company. I work independently and have close contact with the customers. Without actually feeling like an American, I have adapted well to life here. I am no longer a practising Jew, but I feel as Jewish as any Orthodox Jew. The friends I have, like me, were not born in this country and we share a common past. I would have liked to have married, but somehow I never had the courage to go through with it. A young woman once even came from Israel just to see me. I changed my mind at the last moment. I can't explain why I am afraid of making final decisions, but I think the reason lies in my past. I have often regretted not marrying. It would have been nice to have children, but now I am an old Jew and resigned to my fate. I am much more at peace.

I am not really happy but I try to make the best of things although it is not so easy. People here are under pressure and I am not much attracted to the American way of life. I am sure people in Israel are much more involved in their Jewishness and in their own country. I have seriously considered settling there, but I have my job here and my habits are ingrained. Daniel had a sabbatical year there, but it did not go well. I have been a few times. The longer I am there, the more I worry to start all over. Here I have no worries about the future and I earn a good salary. I manage to save some money and I also receive compensation payments from the Germans. I will always manage.

Daniel — The Physicist

Daniel, Meyer's older brother is Professor of Physics at New York University and a strictly observant Jew. He is a modest, yet famous scientist whose advice is widely sought. His father had been deported and died of exhaustion. His oldest brother disappeared and his mother died in Auschwitz.

> In 1943, at the age of 14, I came to the camp with my little 12-year-old brother, Meyer. We stayed together until liberation. I would not be alive if it had not been for Meyer, for he always managed to find some food. He also kept me from losing all hope and, in a way, forced me to survive.
>
> I had always liked mathematics and started studying as soon as I arrived in France. One year later, my friend Elie Wiesel and I tried to pass our baccalaureate certificates but I failed because of my inadequate knowledge of French.
>
> First my brother and I considered leaving on the Exodus, but we went to New York because we found family there. We felt very lonely in New York. Undertaking regular studies was impossible because we did not speak a word of English. I entered a yeshiva and picked up a few words of English here and there. I enrolled at a university in 1949 and worked at odd jobs to pay my way, as a bellboy, delivery boy and errand boy in a drug store. I obtained a degree in physics in 1952, but lacking U.S. citizenship, was unable to find work. So I continued working at the drug store for a few dollars a week. In 1953, five years after my arrival in the United States I became an American citizen, an event that changed my life. Suddenly I obtained a job in the Navy laboratories and kept it for 12 years while pursuing my studies at the university.
>
> I am so grateful to this country for the trust it has placed in me. As soon as I became an American citizen, I was granted clearance and was allowed to do research work in Washington on atomic secrets and existing weaponry. The unrestrictive trust the Americans have for their citizens is very unusual.
>
> I was soon earning well but neither money nor diplomas, degrees or doctorates felt very important to me. I never went to my graduation ceremonies. I believe that my career is an after-

effect of my life in the camps because without that experience I would never have undertaken such worldly studies. Our family had accepted only religious studies. The deportation was a turning point for me. Because I was still so very young, I believe that the camps have had a strong influence on my present day life, although I seldom think of them now. One dream keeps returning. It concerns the last day before liberation when I was hiding in the barracks while others were being shot outside. It reminds me that nothing compares with the fear of the unknown.

In 1955, I married the daughter of a rabbi. From that day on, my social life developed. People respond differently to married men. We have three sons. I don't get too involved in their education, which makes my wife complain I don't do enough upbringing. I feel that they must manage by themselves. They are free to decide to learn or not. I have the same attitude with my students. At the beginning of my lectures, I use the first two times to make an impression with my knowledge and after that I do not interfere.

My students know that I am not from this country because of my accent. I told them that I came from Poland. During the summer, when it is too warm to wear a jacket, they see my tattooed number. I don't hide anything from them but I don't speak openly of it either. I don't discuss the camps with my children in spite of their many questions. I am totally absorbed in my scientific research work and lead a very interesting life.

I usually do not expose so much of myself, but it made me happy that you gave me the opportunity to speak so freely about myself.

Solomon — The Doctor

Upon his arrival in New York, Solomon, now a successful surgeon, had the number that was tattooed on his arm removed, not that he has ever forgotten it

— A3880. He was born in 1928 in Czechoslovakia and was the eldest of four children. His mother, sisters, brother, and grandmother had been taken from the ghetto to unknown destinations. He and his father together were deported to Auschwitz.

> We stayed together for just a few days. I was sent to Guisha, a small camp, where I had to work very hard under the surveillance of young SS soldiers. We had to unload cement bags weighing 200 pounds and carry them along the road. When a prisoner collapsed, the Kapos and SS soldiers killed them with heavy clubs. I was unable to carry a bag by myself and hid when the train with the bags arrived. I knew perfectly well that I would be killed if I were discovered, but believed I had a better chance of surviving trying to hide.
>
> A year and a half after liberation, Niny met a Hungarian in London who was searching for the son of his friend. His friend was my father. He was alive and so was my mother and I had been convinced that all my family had died. Two days before the arrival of the Russians, my father had managed to escape with ten other prisoners into the forest and avoided being evacuated from Auschwitz to Buchenwald, thus escaping a likely death. I wrote them immediately and after reading my letter, my mother fainted.
>
> I visited my parents in Hungary and we resumed the same excellent relationship we had enjoyed before the war. I had received an affidavit from an uncle living in the United States so I did not stay with my parents for very long but promised to have them join me there. I was able to obtain a Canadian visa for them and they settled in Montreal where they still live. My uncle found work for me with a Hungarian Jew. I had to assemble cigarette lighters and I was very unhappy because I could not speak a word of English. I went to evening classes where within one year, I learned to speak fluent English. With the help of scholarships, I studied to become an Industrial

Engineer and graduated in Dallas. I had great difficulties finding a job that allowed me to observe the Sabbath. I wanted to lead a religious life and most of all, I wanted to become independent. I decided to study medicine which would have been impossible without my wife's help. She was a secretary at the stock exchange and worked throughout my pre-medical studies, four years of medical school, and my specialty in plastic surgery. They were long and expensive studies. We waited until I had graduated before having our first child. We now have two children who are observant and receive a religious education.

My orthopaedics and plastic surgery practice is going quite well. I have purchased the building where my offices are located.

Leo Margulies — The Counsellor at Taverny

The members presiding over the dinner party at the reunion were Rabbi Moshe and Mr. Leo Margulies, without whom no commemorative gathering of the former boys of Taverny, nor the wedding of one of their children, would be celebrated.

The former counsellor to the children and adolescents is held in great esteem and his authority accepted since the days of Taverny.

One day in August of 1945, a huge furniture van arrived in Ambloy loaded with used clothing from American Jews. The children were anxious to exchange their striped pyjamas for normal clothing, but Leo Margulies pushed through the crowd, opened the doors of the truck and disappeared inside. Everyone silently accepted that he would be the first to select from the garments because he was the oldest. A long time passed and he did not reappear. The children grew impatient. When he finally emerged from the truck, he told them, "I sorted everything out according to size and category. Now go in and help yourself." As for Mr. Margulies, of course he had not taken anything for himself.

Leo Margulies told me his story in his modest apartment in North Manhattan, the religious section comprised of German Jews.

I was born in 1912 in Nuremberg, Germany. My parents were Polish. There were three children and my father was an invalid. My brother and sister succeeded in leaving for England before the war started but I did not receive my visa until 1939. I kept procrastinating about my departure because I did not want to leave my father behind. Three days after war was declared, I finally decided to leave for Holland, which was still a neutral country at that time, but it was already too late. I was arrested at the border and taken to the prison at Nuremberg. From there I was deported to Buchenwald. Standing with my companions in the tightly packed train, I recited Isaiah's verse VIII, 10: 'They will form projects which will never be realised, they will draw up plans which will fail, for God is with us.'

I was confined with political prisoners in Buchenwald, even though I had been arrested solely for being a Jew. Political prisoners did office work in the camp, but I tried as best as I could to learn a trade and chose the most difficult, but most valuable one — masonry. It was important for me to remain a devout Jew, to light candles on Friday evening, to fast on fast days and to celebrate Jewish holidays. Other prisoners mentioned to me once how surprised they had been to see a tiny Sukkah being erected in the camp courtyard of the political section during the Feast of Tabernacles, and how much it had lifted their morale. Without the help of a calendar, computing the exact dates of Jewish holidays was extremely difficult because they are determined by the lunar cycle. I got totally lost in my calculations, but each time a new transport of Dutch or Hungarian Jews arrived in the camp, they provided me with the information.

Despite the dangers involved, I needed to respect the commandments in order to retain my Jewish identity despite the suffering it brought us. Strange as it may seem, the Jewish Kapos were the ones who actually complicated our attempts to worship. Those in charge widely abused their authority; a foreman or a head of barracks would frequently torment a prisoner until he saw suicide as the only escape and ran into the electric fence that surrounded the camp. Most of the Jewish Kapos disregarded all Jewish traditions. When prisoners said their prayers, the Kapos beat and taunted them calling them 'Talmud.' It was terrible to watch most of the prisoners forced to surrender to the most powerful.

One day, my belief in observance saved my life. I had exchanged a few words with a friend, which was strictly forbidden, and noticed the foreman putting my name in his notebook, which usually meant a death sentence. On the way back a non-Jewish German, a member of "The Friends of the Bible," told the foreman: "This man believes in the Bible," and my name was crossed out.

During my camp life I realised the importance of personal discipline. Whatever the temperature, even if I had to break ice, I washed my entire body in cold water every morning. I still do it now.

We heard what was happening several days before liberation from the political prisoners who listened to the radio and received newspapers. The American troops had advanced to 30 miles from Buchenwald and the Germans were resisting strongly. Not wanting a single Jew to be alive when the Americans arrived, they decided to evacuate Buchenwald. The only road available was to the south and they tried to send all Jewish prisoners from the camp to Dachau. But for once, the SS orders were not obeyed as the political prisoners crossed their plans. My friend got me into the resistance and he had procured insignia other than our yellow stars. In a manner of speaking, we went into hiding and thus escaped the fate of the 26,000 Jews who died either in Dachau or on their way there.

Not more than two hours before liberation there was talk of being systematically destroyed. The Americans arrived on the

28th of Nissan (April 11), the exact date my oldest son was born many years later. To me this was a sign from God.

In 1947, after my stay at Taverny, I joined my brother and sister in England. When the Russians invaded Czechoslovakia in 1948, I panicked at the possibility of a third world war and asked a friend of mine to send me an affidavit for the United States.

Since I was 36 years old when I arrived in the United States, I wanted very much to get married and have children, but first I had to find work. Convinced that the only way to be successful in America was to specialise in a field, I learned to be a cutter. When I married Ruth, she urged me to become an accountant for I was unable to earn enough money without an education and profession. I still work for the same firm now. My wife and I have a true Jewish home and our three sons are very devoted Jews. God is still with us.

9

LIFE JOURNEYS —
FRANCE

S ome of the younger boys at Taverny returned to school, unlike those old enough to go to Paris and learn a trade. They studied French and learned it well and frequently decided to make France their permanent home.

I met with four such children in Paris, who had arrived at Écouis in pairs. One pair were two brothers, Bernard 12 and Victor 15. The others were two inseparable friends, Michel 8 and Jacques 10. Upon their arrival at Écouis, both Jacques and Michel were the size of 5-year-old children. This is their story.

<u>Michel</u>

During Michel's stay at Ambloy, a telegram arrived from the German Red Cross stating "Have just found Michel's mother. She'll arrive tomorrow." The child remained strangely impassive at this news and his comrades lacked enthusiasm as well. When asked why they were not excited, they explained that no one really believes that it is Michel's mother. He cannot remember her and we don't believe that she is still alive. Nevertheless, on the following morning Michel went to the station with a group of his friends to wait for his mother.

A woman did arrive and a tense atmosphere prevailed that evening despite the festive table we had prepared for dinner. Michel listened silently and without emotion to the stories his mother told him about the ghetto. She hugged him, she kissed him, she put him to bed and sat at his bedside until he fell asleep. On the following morning she declared that she had to catch the first train to Paris, to run some errands. Of course I got up to pack Michel's suitcase, but she stopped me and told me not to bother. She stated, "He would only be in my way and I prefer to leave him here."

I realised that the children had instinctively been correct. She was not his mother. She had been a friend of Michel's family and had used the opportunity to get out of Germany. Michel met her again in the United States many years later. He did not blame her for the role she had assumed, given the situation and he became close friends with her. After all, she was the only person who had known his family.

Michel is now in the advertising business and lives in Paris. He married a non-Jewish girl whom he met at the Club Méditerranée. They have two little boys.

Michel explained to me that he owed three things to his wife: his driver's licence, which he finally obtained after many previous failures, the courage to buy an apartment, and his two sons.

In their large living room, family photos were pointed out hanging side by side. One grouping, Michel's wife pointed out as "My family," an engraving of the Western Wall in Jerusalem where Jews say their prayers she said was "Michel's family."

Jacques

As for Jacques, he did find his family. He was in Versailles when he was informed by the OSE that his mother had survived and was living with her two daughters in Munich. Having learned our lesson in the case of Michel's mother, we decided not to have her come to us, but to send Jacques to her during summer vacation. The trip was very stressful for him. He did not remember his mother and he had no idea how to behave. He felt at ease with her when he arrived in Munich, yet his uncertainty persisted. Only during the Sabbath, when his mother lit the candles and prepared the traditional dishes did the memory of his childhood and the mother he had lost return to him. His anxieties vanished.

Jacques' mother later came to France with the assistance of the OSE, and with only one of her daughters, the other having been married in the meantime. The two women worked as seamstresses making skirts in a tiny room. At night Jacques' sister studied for her diploma. Once he was able to afford it, Jacques rented an apartment for his mother and did not want her to work any longer. He invited me to her place one evening and asked her to sing for me. She sang a song in Yiddish that contained the following words: "Be quiet, my child. If the Germans hear you cry, they'll find us and we'll all be killed. Hush, hush, my child." Jacques is now a well-known physician and specialist in psychoanalysis.

Michel and Jacques, because of their inseparable bond to one another, told their stories together as part of a dialogue between them.

> **Michel:** "I was born in Piotrkow, Poland, where we lived next door to the rabbi. Lulek, his youngest son, was the same age as I. We both worked in the ghetto in the glass factory for the Germans. We were four years old and had to bring water to the glass blowers who were always thirsty. The factory stayed open night and day and the crew worked in eight-hour shifts. When night came and I was unable to keep my eyes open any longer I would build a shelter out of empty boxes and fall asleep. The German guards always found me and threw buckets of cold water on me to wake me up. Lulek and I met again in Buchenwald. He saved his brother's life a few days before liberation by hiding him in our barracks.
>
> **Jacques:** I had also hidden under a mattress with my father. He died shortly after liberation.
>
> **Michel:** I wasn't staying with my father, but managed to see him every evening. It gave me a sense of security.
>
> **Jacques:** Which barracks was he in?
>
> **Michel:** Number 62. I stayed there for one week. Half the people died there every night. Then he was transferred to a brick barracks and I to Number 8. You and your father were in barracks 66. I was only eight years old but I remember it very well. A child of eight during that time was the same as a 20 year old today. The only thing I knew at liberation was that one could die of hunger.
>
> **Jacques:** On liberation day I heard shots and executions on the outside and a noise from a siren different than I had heard before. People were saying that the Americans were coming and

they would parachute bread one yard long to us. I looked up to the sky to see if this bread was already falling.

I often wondered whether it would not have been better for the little ones to have stayed with a family rather than in a children's home, so I posed that question to Jacques and Michel.

Jacques: Not necessarily. I think that people would have thought concentration camp children to be weird. Slipping all sorts of food into their pockets while there was enough to eat would not have been accepted or understood by those who had not lived in the camps. Being among our peers at least gave us a sense of security. Niny mentioned to me once that we did not know how to play, that we were just sitting around all day as if we were mentally handicapped. At least we were all alike, we did not differ from the others.

Michel: We did not speak a word of French during the first few months and were fortunate to have a very gentle teacher at our school, Madame Wassel-Lacroix. In my first dictation I made 74 mistakes and there were only 74 words.

Jacques: The period of adjustment lasted a year or two. We learned to speak French well and in the company of others we became children again.

Michel: I remember my bar mitzvah in Versailles. I received a watch and roller skates as gifts. I tried out my roller skates the next day, fell, and broke my watch. Most people thought that only small children lived in the children' homes and therefore I got all the shoes they sent. I owned seventeen pairs and took them along in a sack from one home to the next. Shoes are very important to a Jew. Having shoes could save your life in the camps. I also got a huge pair of pants in Ambloy, so large that using some pocket money I had two pairs made, one long and one short.

Jacques: What Michel said is true, to a Jew shoes are the most important thing. I am always scared that our little boy might lose his shoes. I once woke up with a nightmare during our vacation fearing that I had lost my son's shoes.

We were at that time the youngest and we changed the most in the children's home. It was in Ambloy that we were together with our Buchenwald friends. Later, the littlest went to Versailles while the older ones stayed at Taverny. That was awful for us because you and Niny were like mothers to us. The fear of loss of love was so great for the youngest. In Taverny there was a kind of family life, complete with brothers. That's why we came back so often.

In the children's home there was a big difference between the war orphans and some children with social problems. It is a pity we were thrown together simply because we were of the same age. Age should not have been the determinant. We were clearly more mature than the others.

At age 18 we were sent away to be on our own. It was a strict rule. I couldn't go to my mother because she was still too poor even to buy bread every two days. I helped her with my allowance.

It was a difficult time. I was reasonably independent but felt alone, no longer part of a community.

I achieved my high school diploma while still in Versailles. Even in the earliest grades Michel and I were determined to continue our studies, but we didn't know how. I wanted to go straight for my doctoral programme and went to see Professor Kastler, who was connected with the École Normale in the Rue d'Ulm. He told me he could not help me because I wasn't French, so I had to find another course. I reported myself to Supelec (a famous high school), but no one helped us and that was difficult.

Michel: In 1962 I gave up my studies. I felt lonely. I was studying with the help of a scholarship. I had a room, but I felt sad and had little contact with anyone. Finally, I had enough of studying and taking examinations. Some acquaintances helped me get started in the advertising business. It gave me contact with people and I still work there.

Jacques: I sometimes ask myself if I ever truly integrated. Except for my profession, I always have the feeling that I live a little bit to the side, although objectively seen that is not true. That may not have come from the war only, but also what happened before and after. The only time that I did not feel myself an outcast was in May 1968. I was actively involved and stood at the barricades on Rue d'Ulm.

Michel: I did not stand at the barricades, I had other problems. With my work I needed to have money coming in. When the mail went on strike it was a disaster for me, no work, no money. We handled all business over the telephone and had to walk to our clients.

Jacques: After the birth of my oldest son I felt more accepted into the community. I kept myself busy with my professional responsibilities. Perhaps in truth, we did not really want to be entirely integrated into the community.

I met the two couples again on their vacation in Israel in 1983. Michel went to Yad Vashem to show his sons his history because they were already old enough to begin to understand. He was surprised to see a huge photo of himself that read "The youngest survivor of the camps." Then they planted two trees in the forest dedicated to those who perished, in memory of his parents. His wife had saved money for that purpose.

Victor

Victor was of small stature and very active. He was 15 when he came to Écouis and was inseparable from his 12-year-old brother. They were from Poland, had been for a long time in the ghetto and then deported.

The two brothers were transferred to the OSE home in Versailles, but they came to spend weekends and holidays at Taverny until it closed. Victor offered me this account.

> I was born in Streminice, Poland, in 1932 where the two brothers Daniel and Meyer also lived, as well as two brothers who now live in the United States. I was the oldest of three children, my younger brother Bernard, and my little sister who was deported with my mother. I think of them often. My mother was an exceptional person. She had the opportunity to leave the ghetto but refused to leave her elderly mother, who lived with them. My father was with us in Buchenwald. A few days before our liberation, he was taken from the camp and never seen again.
>
> While at Taverny and in Versailles, everyone wanted me to learn leather craft but as a child I was interested in locks and metals. So I registered with ORT in Saules Street in October 1947. The required study including a three-year apprenticeship seemed to me like a lifetime so I made up my mind to join others and take my little brother to Palestine. We stayed for six weeks in Marseilles, boarded the Exodus, and made the voyage which resulted in our being blocked from entry and returned to France via Germany. It was just before the proclamation of the State of Israel in 1948. I was 17, old enough to be a soldier, but they wanted me to come without my brother. I refused. I had done everything humanly possible in the camps to stay with him. I would not leave him now. I returned to the ORT in Paris and they allowed me to finish my first year despite my long absence. I worked through my vacation, took the full three years as well as five years of night courses in industrial arts. The Director of ORT helped me secure a position as a foreman in Montreuil where I worked for twelve years until my boss retired. Then I went to work for myself.
>
> In 1956 I met Alice, a member of an established French-Jewish family. Her mother was deported and killed, her father

died soon after the war. My marriage made me feel more French because of her background. I do not hide my background, I am not ashamed of it. Even though I changed my name and gave our children French names, I kept the Shabbat, registered our children in religious school and we attend synagogue.

I think I am quite well. I used to dream but not any more. The camps left me with the ability to quickly assess people. I know who I will deal with and who not. I don't speak of the camps to the children. I don't think they are interested but I have told them about the Exodus.

I met Victor again in Paris over the years. He had become a French citizen and spoke perfect French with only a trace of an accent. He was increasingly successfull in business. He was no longer religious but his three sons, who were very bright students, all had a bar mitzvah.

On a later visit, Victor admitted to nightmares. He also cannot stand anyone with authority over him. Anything authoritarian makes him very angry.

Because of his love of Écouis, he bought a country house nearby and invites all his friends to visit. In some ways, he remains lonely, preferring the company of his brother and his former comrades from Taverny whom he visits in France and in Israel. At a wedding in Israel of the son of a Taverny friend, Victor felt especially joyful. I saw him there and he indeed looked very happy.

LIFE JOURNEYS —
ISRAEL

Naphtali — The Diplomat

The older brother of the little boy Lulek, who protected his luggage with a toy gun in the Port of Haifa in 1945, has become Consul General for Israel overseas. Although he had no specific political affiliations, he accepted a civil service job in the Ministry of Defense as Assistant to Moshe Dayan and then followed the Minister to the Ministry for Foreign Affairs. Naphtali told me that if my aim was to show that the consequences of concentration camp life make it impossible to lead a normal life, that I would be wrong as far as his life was concerned. And yet, the account demonstrates that like for many of his comrades, his life would have taken an entirely different direction had the war not intervened.

His father was Chief Rabbi of the community of Piotrkow in Poland, where out of the 60,000 inhabitants, more than 26,000 were Jews. The rabbi was an outstanding personality, the 37th descendant of a renowned rabbinical dynasty. He had a Doctorate in Philosophy from the University of Vienna, spoke many languages and had written numerous articles and books. The rabbi had started writing his last book in 1935, a legal discussion about one's behaviour under persecution and towards informers. Naphtali kept the manuscript throughout his hiding places, but eventually lost it.

> I was 13 years old when war was declared. I had four brothers, one of whom had left for Rumania shortly before the war. Except for him, we met again in 1939 in a ghetto where no one was allowed to leave without permission.
>
> Although my father was aware of the coming danger and

could have fled in time, as a rabbi he felt he had the moral duty to remain with the members of his congregation regardless of circumstances. Between October 14 and 21, 1942, 24,000 Jews from Piotrkow were herded into cattle cars. My mother went into hiding in a bunker with my little brother Lulek. My father refused to do so because he worried that if the Germans could not find the rabbi, they would search all the bunkers and capture those who were in hiding. He was deported with all the others, as was my oldest brother. After this round up, all Jews who worked and lived on the outside like me were forced back into the ghetto. There were now only about 2,000 of us left and the ghetto had become a camp surrounded with barbed wire. A community kitchen was established which was run by my mother.

When the Russian army approached our town in 1944, we were deported to Germany. We were taken to a camp near the border and the women were sent on to Ravensbrück. At the last possible moment, I tore Lulek out of my mother's arms. He was seven years old and stayed with me at the camp installed for the Hassag Werke, a factory for the repair of tanks. I left him in the barracks when I had to leave for work. He received the same food as everyone else but from time to time people threw him extra breadcrumbs or peelings.

I have an optimistic nature that did not change even during deportation. Yet, I was sure I would never see my father or any of my family again. I am still not quite sure of what my feelings were then. What did I learn in the camps? I learned to survive.

At the time of the evacuation of Buchenwald, Lulek ended up in Barracks No. 8 with privileged senior inmates, the old timers. From there, he was brought to Barracks 66 where Gustav was the head. He led a command of men whose mission was to punish informers by strangling them. One week before liberation, the Germans assembled us two or three times a day for roll call (Appel). They were preparing for our evacuation. The first time on Appel, I saw a friend of mine lying dead in a trench. No longer having shoes, I wanted to take his, but he stirred very slightly and whispered "lie down next to me."

Three days later I was driven from the camp with other comrades and taken to the train station. During the night I jumped off the train with two others, but instead of hiding, I walked for two days and nights back towards Buchenwald. I did not want to lose Lulek. The Americans liberated the camp three days later. I contracted typhus and Lulek had the measles.

It took us five weeks to recover from our illnesses and then we left for France. I wanted my little brother to gain back his strength before taking him to the Holy Land. Our parents and older brother had disappeared, but we rejoiced in finding our fourth brother, Chiko, who was already in Palestine.

I volunteered for the Hagana and entered training. I planned to go the Hebrew University in Jerusalem but gave up the idea because studying seemed too long and complicated. In order to regain peace of mind, I decided to study at a yeshiva and chose one situated in the countryside at Petach Tikva. I needed long walks and to be in touch with nature. I spent 2½ years there, first reviewing what I had already learned before. I asked no one for help.

During vacations I worked in the nearby orange plantations. I was not a typical yeshiva student, the kind who sits for hours at a time studying the Talmud. As a member of the Haganah, I participated in the illegal landing operations. I felt completely adjusted to life in Israel and I did not experience anything unusual or abnormal in the process.

At first I thought that I had lost the best years of my life during the war. But when I was about 23 years old, I realised that I was also more mature than other young people my age due to my experiences in the camps and so these were good years for me.

I did not get married until 1956 when I felt financially

secure working as a journalist. My wife and I have four children and I feel very close to them. My youngest son often visits his uncle Lulek who talks more freely about the past than I do. When he returns from his visits, he frequently asks me to confirm the accuracy of certain incidents and anecdotes.

Naphtali's wife told me how emotional he became while covering the Eichman trial as an official journalist. He suffered nightmares and retreated into silence. She sought the advice of a psychologist who suggested that he meet with former inmates. Talking about the camps did indeed help Naphtali to feel better again. He considers himself a normal father but his wife does recall how upset he was when his oldest son entered the army and he heard of the long marches the young soldiers had to endure. Naphtali states that he is leading a completely normal and satisfying life in the Holy Land. Still, at times, he admits to feeling somewhat different from native Israelis.

Other people make plans, strive for success, while I have the impression that I have achieved more than I could ever have hoped for and will do nothing extraordinary to improve my status. I must be the only person in Israel who has never asked for an increase or a bonus. I am happy with what I have. I occasionally think about getting a promotion but would not take great pains to obtain one. I have been successful in my job because I conscientiously carry out the tasks given to me just as my parents taught me to do. My children, true to the religious tradition of their ancestors, display the same attitude. This is most important to me.

Alex — The Army Officer

Alex was 15 years old when he arrived in Taverny, but he looked 12. On Shabbat, we asked him to sing "Shaeffele," a Yiddish song about a shepherd who lost his sheep but recovered them with the help of God. Eventually, we ended up calling him "Shaeffele" and soon no one remembered him as Alex.

I met him accidentally in Tel Aviv. A tall man with blue eyes and white hair came up to me and asked me if my name was Judith. It was Alex. We sat down to chat and he was eager to talk.

Alex —
the army Officer

I was born in Rumania in 1930,the youngest of eight children.
My parents were already 45 years old at my birth. We were very
poor but none of the beggars who knocked at our door were ever
sent away empty-handed. Our house was spotless and
sparkling clean. Even the two-handled bowl with which we
used to wash our hands before meals was polished and shining
at all times. Thanks to the habits of cleanliness, I was able to
survive the camps. I always tried to stay clean and washed in
cold water every day.

We spoke Yiddish and Rumanian at home and I studied at
the heder. When war broke out, everyone was first confined to a
ghetto. Then all the Jews of our little town, half of the total
population, were sent to Auschwitz-Birkenau. I was separated
from my family and sent to work at a construction site. It was
very difficult work. Elie Wiesel and I were together the entire
time. We were from the same place and had known each other
before the war.

A German gave me the nickname "Der Kleine trottel" (little
idiot, an expression not to be taken literally for it often had a
sympathetic connotation). In fact, he liked me and gave me a
piece of bread when I left for work every morning.

Later I was put in Barracks 66 in Buchenwald. When the
Germans tried to make us leave the barracks three days before
liberation, all those who realised what was going on hid
wherever they could. I sought refuge in the sewers under our
barracks. I held onto a ladder for three days and nights, without
food or water. Every 20 yards there were ladders with others
clinging to them. The Americans finally arrived and gave me a
whole loaf of bread. Afraid that I wouldn't get any more, I saved
part of it, an act that may have saved my life. Many others died
of overeating.

I have wonderful memories of Ambloy and of Niny who took
me with her to Bretagne, where she was in charge of a holiday
camp. Shortly before leaving for the United States, I received a

letter from my older sister, who had survived the camps and lived in Antwerp. Without saying a word to anyone, I left to stay with her and her husband. She took care of me like a mother. While in Belgium, I gave up the idea of going to America and joined Betar, a very nationalistic Jewish youth movement. My dream was to participate in the struggle to create a Jewish country. At age 17, I embarked on the "Altalena," the ship which carried arms for the Irgun, a clandestine nationalistic movement whose leader was Menachem Begin. The Altalena was sunk just off Tel Aviv on Ben-Gurion's orders.

Eager to fight for my country, I volunteered for a combat unit shortly after I arrived. Once in the army, I started growing like a mushroom and am now over 6 feet tall. I kept to myself and did not search for my friends from Taverny. I would go to Tel Aviv during leave, buy a falafel and a bottle of soda and sit on a shaded bench on Rothschild Boulevard. I was happy. I would return to my quarters in the evening.

Two years after I had become a soldier, the military police were created. They recruited tall men particularly and I stayed with them until I retired at age 52, reaching the rank of Colonel.

When I was 23 years old, I met a woman soldier of Rumanian origin but who had not been deported. I married her. She is a nurse now and her parents, especially her mother, are wonderful to me. We have two children, a son who works at the Ministry of Defense and a married daughter. I never speak about the camps to them, but they know everything for they have read every book on the subject. I realise that I react to my children with too much affection. My daughter, who lives close by, recently had a baby. Once a day she calls to tell me that she has just prepared the baby's bath. At that point I drop everything and run over there. I hold my granddaughter's little feet and I am overwhelmed with happiness.

I tried to suppress the past for a long time. The only item I saved are the pants I wore when I was deported. I cut off the legs to make gym shorts out of them. I was about to throw them away when they became too tight and suddenly realised they were the only remaining tie to my parents, so I kept them. I wash them myself and never show them to anyone.

Nowadays the past is constantly on my mind. I have nightmares and I think of my parents more frequently than before. Now that I can afford it, I wish I could spoil my mother just once and repay her for the sweetness and kindness she brought into my life.

I am content with my life. At the time of liberation I never thought my life would turn out so well. I was put in charge of the military prisoners. Considering my past, this may seem strange, but it is precisely because of my past experiences that I have always made efforts to ease the situation of the prisoners. Whenever I proposed a lessening of punishment, my request was always given serious consideration and often implemented.

I had not left Israel since I arrived here in 1947 until three years ago when the army sent me to the NATO countries to study the methods of various military prisons. Aware that Germany was a member of NATO, I was very reluctant to go and consulted with a rabbi who told me that this trip was part of my duties. All went well until I arrived in Germany. I became terribly scared and requested an interpreter from the Israeli embassy. German officers lined both sides of the staircase leading to the offices. Sweat poured down my face. Without the interpreter present I think I would have fainted. I was asked to sign their guest register. Most of the participants had written to thank them for the perfect arrangements. I simply wrote in Hebrew, "I heard your deliberations." The official part of my job was over. One of the German officers, having heard the translation of my comment from the interpreter said to me, "You have been such an attentive listener that I believe that you understand German very well." The interpreter translated my answer from Hebrew, "That's right, I understand German perfectly." "Then why did you ask for an interpreter?" asked the German officer. I rolled up my sleeve and showed my camp number. Immediately there was a chorus of voices exclaiming that no one there had anything to do with it and that all were too young to have participated, it was the older generation. They asked me if they could take me out and I answered "Zum Bahnhof" (to the station). By the time I reached Paris to meet my wife, I was completely shattered.

I am no longer practicing the Jewish religion since I do not believe that God is concerned about the fate of humankind. Still, I am convinced that a core of devout Jews must carry on as in the past and ensure the continuity of Jewish traditions. While in the army, I supported the exemption of yeshiva students from military service.

Martin — The Carpenter

Martin's face contrasted sharply with the pale complexions of the other boys of Taverny. He looked like a little farm boy with rosy red cheeks, making him look like a 13 year old, rather than his actual age of 16. His healthy looks had caused him to receive even smaller rations than his comrades at Buchenwald. He had come to the camp of Yavichewitz at age 13 and was forced to work in the coal mines, standing 12 hours at a time without rest. His father worked in the same mine until he grew so weak that he was taken to the gas chambers. One Sunday, the SS carried a cartload of wet mouldy bread from the kitchen. One of the prisoners walked over to it and then the others followed. Watching big men fighting for bread that would not have been fed to the pigs in his hometown was a horrible sight and he swore to himself never to become like those poor, famished creatures.

Because of my chubby cheeked looks, I never received an extra piece of bread and soon became a 'Mussulman.' When I pushed the skin of my feet with my finger, a dent would remain there for

at least one hour. A Czechoslovakian doctor told me that I
needed vitamins but that he didn't have any. Although my feet
were covered with red and black spots, I continued to drag
myself to work. To this day, I don't understand how I was able to
run to the gate when the Americans arrived, as I wasn't even
able to walk. Their presence seemed to heal me. I was terribly
bitter and thought that the whole world would rise to avenge
our suffering. But instead, the Americans protected the German
soldiers, bringing them food and scolding us when we spat at

Martin the carpenter

them. The American Jewish soldiers who understood our reactions were assigned elsewhere. It made me realise that there are different brotherhoods, one amongst Jews, another amongst non-Jews.

Having heard from Arie, who had worked with me in the coal mines, that there was a country for Jews called Palestine, I decided to learn a trade and then live there and fight for our own country. I chose carpentry because I remembered a sickly boy of my age who lived in my hometown in Hungary. His mother sent him to work for a carpenter. He had to gather branches and tree stumps from the forest, saw them and make furniture from them. He became big and strong. When he was with us, the non-Jewish boys were afraid of him. He was my ideal.

Martin tried to leave for Palestine as quickly as possible, but despite his desire to go and fight, Mr. Margulies prevented him from leaving until he had obtained proper visas for both Martin and Arie in 1946.

During the wait Martin had a revelation. He had been invited to lunch in a restaurant on the Rue des Rosiers. Some Jewish women dining there, who knew that he had survived Buchenwald, came over to him and asked him whether it was true that there was almost nothing to eat in the camps. He confirmed it and they started crying. He found it strange that people would cry over his not having enough to eat when the real problem was having lost his parents and seven brothers and sisters.

At that time I decided never to mention it to anyone again. Other people simply cannot understand. That is when I cut all links to my past.

When, at age 18, I finally arrived in Jerusalem, I went to all the carpenters in town and asked the best among them to hire me. When someone mentioned that they only paid two pounds per week and whether that was enough, I replied that I had not asked about my salary, but about work.

My dream was to live in a village, in a kibbutz, but circumstances led me to enter the Navy. As a frogman I accepted any mission. But when I was just about to sign a contract, I was asked whether as a practising Jew. I might have a problem with accepting a mission on the Sabbath.

I had felt like a brother to my colleagues and was deeply hurt by that question which concerned my loyalty so I didn't sign up. I returned to Jerusalem and worked as a carpenter. I had no aspirations to become rich but I did want to be independent and earn enough money to marry and have a family, which I did when I was 35 years old.

While in the camp, I had always dreamed about my family and this continued after liberation. When no one returned I was terribly depressed. I recently dreamt that I was repairing a room in our old family home, but instead of living in the completed part of the house, I stayed in the room I was fixing. Suddenly, a stranger entered and my parents also appeared at the same time. I awakened from my dream and saw my entire family before me. This made me very happy. Clearly there was a link between my trade and my childhood.

Despite my disappointment with the Navy, I remained a fervent patriot. However, I hold no hatred against the Arabs or towards the Germans. But I do like to keep my distance from them. In my mind, revenge was never an option.

Arie — The Nationalist

Arie's father, a prosperous grocery store owner in a small town in Ruthenia, was not a Zionist. Arie's much-loved older brother had joined the youth movement of the B'nei Akiva and so he followed his brother's example and became a passionate believer in the idea of the Holy Land as a permanent home.

One day I used all of my pocket money to buy a map of Palestine from a friend. My parents became frightened when the Germans occupied our town and asked me to give them the map. I refused and took it to bed with me. That night my father took it and burned it, an incident which I recall still with bitterness.

The non-Jewish population of our town was very hostile. A boy threatened me one day accusing me that I had killed his God. One of the school teachers called a friend of mine a dirty Jew. I was only a little boy of eight at the time, but I already knew the meaning of anti-Semitism.

In April 1944, my entire family, my parents and their four children, were deported to Auschwitz. Upon arrival, Doctor Mengele sent my father to the left, to the gas chambers. I was about to follow him but the doctor motioned me to the right, even though I was small and very thin. The Germans beat us unmercifully, pushing us towards the barracks. I cried. Another boy, barely older than myself, reprimanded me and told me that if I wanted to stay alive I had better stop crying and pull myself together. He warned me to be strong, as despair would not get me anywhere. He also advised me to get a number tattooed on my arm and to try and get out of Auschwitz as quickly as possible. He appeared to me like a vision of Elijah the prophet and, thanks to him, I regained my self-control.

I was transferred to Yavichewitz, to work in the coal mines with other young boys. I continued to dream about Palestine and life on a kibbutz. In my mind I saw a large communal group of houses surrounding a wide yard called Eretz Israel. It was the hope of living there some day that sustained me, but the details of concentration camp life have also remained engraved in my memory.

There were non-Jewish Poles working the camp kitchens who, having heard that there were children among the prisoners, decided to share some of their more plentiful rations with us. I couldn't eat the horse meat because it disgusted me, so I exchanged it for potatoes. This might have saved my life at the time of liberation. We had not eaten for three days and were literally starving to death. The Americans gave us meat, but I was unable to swallow it and only ate potatoes, which prevented me from getting sick.

Some of the Germans were very sadistic, constantly inflicting new cruelties on us. One day, during an alarm, the electricity was cut off and a young Jew from our barracks seized the opportunity to escape over the otherwise electrified fence. He lived in the nearby forest like a wild animal, sneaking up to the villages during night time to steal food, but was soon recaptured. The Germans interrupted our work and made us assemble in the large courtyard around the pole that held the gong which sounded morning reveille. There we were forced to watch the young fugitive hanged. We had to march past the dead body and repeat the phrase 'This is the punishment that awaits an escapee.'

The Germans debased and degraded us to a point where we lost our human dignity. One Sunday, our only day of rest, an SS officer attached a piece of bread to the end of a string. He threw this bread into the air and watched as hundreds of prisoners jumped up and down in attempts to grab it. Then to top it off, the soldier set his German Shepherd dog against the poor, famished prisoners.

It was in the camp that I decided never to live with non-Jews. My decision was reaffirmed by an incident that took place right after liberation from Buchenwald. A young communist had assembled all the children to make a political speech. He urged us to return to our country in order to participate in the communist struggle. When we continued to chat, he exclaimed 'What is going on here? Is this a synagogue of some kind?' This of course strengthened our conviction not to join him.

All of these memories returned at the time of the Eichman trial. It was during a military training period. The sergeant asked us to put away the ammunition after a manoeuvre. I heaved the box on my shoulders while many other soldiers just stood around talking. Noticing them, the sergeant said 'Now I can understand Eichman. You are all lazy and spoiled.' I dropped the box and screamed in rage 'I've heard that somewhere before!' I complained to a higher-ranking officer who made the sergeant apologise to me.

During the battle for the old city of Jerusalem in 1948, the Jewish soldiers had arrested a few Arabs from the Katamon section. They separated the men who were old enough to fight, from the women and children, grabbing one of the Arabs away from his youngsters who cried, 'Papa! Papa!' Old memories surfaced and I turned away to hide my tears. Later, when an older soldier and I were guarding Arab suspects, one of the prisoners asked to step outside to relieve himself. He was told by the older soldier to do it right there and I argued that since he was not armed and we were, why not just accompany him outside. He refused. Again I felt sick and turned away so he would not notice my being upset.

After the war I had tuberculosis and was not able to learn a trade in France. As soon as I was healed I left for Palestine with my friend Martin. I was very disappointed when I realised that no one was going to pay any special attention to me, whether in the reception home of Atlit, or in the big city of Tel Aviv, or at Kfar Saba, where I went to join Martin.

I had gone to the yeshiva Kol-Torah in Jerusalem, but I think it was a mistake. I joined the Haganah and the non-political youth movement, the Ezra. I wanted to meet as many Sabras as possible. I was terribly lonely until joined by my brother from Italy, who had survived the camps also. He intended to live in Jerusalem, which was still under British control at the time, but because of the unemployment there went to Haifa.

I joined the army to participate in the War for Independence. The director of my yeshiva asked me why I wanted to fight, given that all my family had been murdered. I replied simply

'The fate of my people is also my fate.' I was shot in the lungs and recuperated in a hospital for three months.

After my release, I wanted to become a printer and receive a better education to make up for the many years I had lost. Aware that there was a lack of teachers, I took a preparatory course and was sent to teach in a village school. Having to deal with undisciplined children was very difficult for me and I was again extremely lonely. In 1954, at age 26, I married a sabra of Russian-Polish descent. I began to feel better and tried to give my oldest son the many opportunities I had missed.

I think I am more nationalistic than other Israelis and I am also more critical of the shortcomings of my country. It is very important to me to remember the deportations and to add to that memory a nationalistic dimension by stressing the importance of the State of Israel.

Aron — The Artist

After receiving the news that his little brother Uri was found alive in Germany, Aron immediately left Taverny to find him. They left together for Palestine as soon as they could.

Aron had been very happy as a child in Ruthenia (a former province of Czechoslovakia), but in 1941 his father was sent East with the Hungarian army and never returned. The family was penniless one year later when Aron was nearly 15. He left for Budapest to work with a trucker who allowed him to share his apartment. When the Germans occupied Hungary in 1943, Aron tried to escape into Yugoslavia with a friend, but they were caught at the border and sent to Auschwitz.

I was shocked when I arrived at the camp. I was furious at the Hungarian Jewish leaders who must have known what was going on but did not tell us. I was soon transferred to Magdeburg, another camp located close to a chemical factory. The prisoners had to clean up the filthy work done there. Food was insufficient. I wouldn't have survived if I had not been resourceful and found ways to exchange vitamins from Red Cross supplies for bread or other food with privileged non-Jewish prisoners and the politicals. The Germans wanted to annihilate the Jews but did not hate each of us personally. I was young then and the guards did not scare me. I was sure that once I had come out of this hell, everything would be the same as before. I would return to my hometown, to my mother and to my family. I thought of nothing else.

Two months before liberation we were evacuated to Buchenwald. There I tore the yellow star off my uniform and replaced it with a 'T' standing for Czechoslovakian. I went into hiding until liberation but lived in a constant state of terror. It was awful.

After the war, and having found my younger brother, we embarked for Palestine on the Exodus but were sent back to Hamburg where we spent three more months in a displaced persons camp. Then we left once more for Israel with false passports.

I arrived in Israel during the War of Independence and joined the army. I was a fireman with mine clearing soldiers and was very happy. We were no longer treated like animals. We were brave Jews defending our country.

After leaving the army, I worked as a mechanic for a construction firm in Haifa, but when the project was finished, I had no work. For a while I lived in a home for demobilised soldiers and then found a job in the port, refurbishing a ship, which was to bring new immigrants to Israel. Once this job was done I was at a new impasse.

By now I was completely fed up, not with working fourteen hours a day, but with not having steady work. I joined the police force and was very much influenced by its three-month training course. Our Scottish instructor brought us British discipline, insisting on properly made beds, a regular morning inspection, and even table manners. I needed this to resign myself to life's demands.

I married and had two children. It was not a good marriage but my wife and I decided not to divorce for the sake of the children. She could not get used to my being a policeman with unpredictable working hours.

After 10 years of marriage, I left the police force and became a boat mechanic.

After 6½ years there, I realised that I had no future and was ready to give up. I wanted to be independent and opened a small pipe manufacturing company just before the Six-Day War, at the height of the crisis. Of course it did not work out and I took a job in the factory where I work to this day. Everybody wants to be his own boss but how does one make it happen?

We eventually divorced and my wife has since remarried. My sister-in-law, who does not approve of divorce, refuses to see me and prevents me from seeing my own brother.

I often suffer depressions like I did in Taverny and at times I have problems with my heart. It is because my heart has hardened. Sometimes it swells up and then shrinks again. It makes me afraid. It is very depressing. I haven't been to a doctor because I don't need one to know what these crises are. I cannot stand anyone upsetting me or questioning my honour.

I never mention the past because I don't want people to feel sorry for me. But whether I talk about it or not, subconsciously I am always thinking of the camps. I was very happy when Eichman was caught. Revenge at last! I wish many more would be caught as well. I read every newspaper report about proceedings against German war criminals.

I lost the best years of my life in the camps. I was terribly frightened for my son during the Yom Kippur War. I couldn't have endured losing him. Every day I prayed to die in his place. I prayed to God not to let him die in his nineteenth year before

having had a chance to live. I am definitely in favour of peace,
even to the point of making concessions.

In the meantime, Aron has started to paint and has found relief in his new
occupation. He paints the changing nature of the sea and has had success in
exhibitions.

Aron carried a violent hatred within himself, hate against his own
Hungarian community for not having warned him and hate against himself for
not having resisted more actively. In Israel, where he was given the opportunity
to prove his strength by helping to build a new State and fighting in its army, he
has managed to readjust to life. It proved to be the best place for him.

Eli — The Teacher

Eli was a quiet, gentle boy with large melancholy eyes. Because he was 14 years
old when he arrived at Taverny, I sent him to school. He quit after the first day
and adamantly refused to go back. He was the son of a rabbi of a small
Hungarian town. There were six children in his family. He and his older brother,
Mendel, were the only ones to survive.

> We never read the newspapers at home and yet my father
> always seemed to know what was going on and what lay in
> store for the Polish Jews. But as a Hungarian, he never thought
> that anything would happen to us.
>
> So when the Hungarians arrested us one Sunday during the
> Jewish Passover, we did not think it was serious. Each family
> was given a horse cart onto which we loaded our belongings to
> move to the ghetto. At each halt, we had to leave behind some
> bags with our names tagged to them. Thirty-five days after we
> were arrested, the police ordered us to leave all our baggage. It
> was on Shabbat, and I did not have to follow the
> commandments strictly for I was not yet 13 years old. Therefore
> I wrote our new address on the tags that the police had given us.
> We were then crowded into cattle wagons with tiny, wired

windows. What I remember most about our three-day journey was the little baby in my mother's arms screaming for something to drink.

We arrived in Auschwitz-Birkenau in the evening and had to remain in the train for another night. On the following morning, prisoners in striped pyjamas opened the doors. I was horrified at what I saw, yet at the same time impressed by the obvious organisation of the Germans. I remember a Dr. Fischer, who held the same rank as Dr. Mengele. The two doctors oversaw the arrival of 10,000 Jews each day, never losing their good manners when greeting new prisoners.

My father appeared before Dr. Fischer, who asked his age. Aware of what was happening, my father answered, "I am 46 years old, but I am still able to work." He spoke in German, as he had been Chief Rabbi in Karlsbad and Marienbad. Dr. Fischer said to him, "Show me your hands," and after inspecting them, sent him to the right. My brother Mendel, a very strong boy, was also sent to the right. Standing between the two, tightly holding onto their hands, I was able to slip through. The doctor said nothing.

We were sent to Yavichewitz to work in the coal mines. My father worked underground mining coal. At the end of the conveyor belt, above ground, 42 children and adolescents had to clean the stones and dirt from the coal. It was far less difficult work than that which my brother was forced to do. One day, my father fell sick and Dr. Fischer promised to send him and the other sick prisoners to a hospital. We never saw him again and Mendel and I never again spoke about him.

Dr. Fischer was a very elegant man and often came into our barracks. He once distributed pills to the 42 children, but we were afraid of being poisoned and refused to swallow them. Dr. Fischer very delicately took a pill out of the box and swallowed it. This convinced us that they were in fact, vitamins, and we agreed to take them.

I met Martin, a Hungarian, who was my age and we occasionally recited the Gemara (Talmudic commentary). These were always very special days. Most of the time, however, I thought of nothing but food. One day we received from Auschwitz some crusts of bread cooked in jam. They were so delicious that we planned to try the recipe after the war.

Mendel was quick to learn how to get along but I was just a "Schlemazel," a clumsy fellow. I survived only because I was too small to do hard work and because we had a fairly clean camp.

In 1945, as the Russians were advancing, we were all evacuated from Yavichewitz and forced to walk to Buchenwald. I was too weak and Mendel carried me most of the way. We were separated when we arrived in Buchenwald. The children's barracks seemed fairly good to me. The daily rations were the same as in Yavichewitz but I did not have to work. I was glad that I did not have to leave the barracks because Buchenwald was so large it appeared overwhelming to me. One evening, long after our arrival, someone entered the children's barracks and said to me that he was my brother.

He looked like a skeleton with eyes. I did not recognize him. He was unable to see or to hear and was too thin to even sit down. He had been working outside of the camp and unless he returned by 6:00 o'clock in the evening, the Germans would kill him. One evening returning late to the barracks, he begged the Germans to let him in. They grabbed a big piece of wood and hit him on the head and shoved him savagely through the gate. One of the prisoners helped him to our barracks. One of the boys, who had gone to a relative in another barracks, left a piece of bread. Everyone craved it, but the head of our table gave it to my brother. On the following day, one very exceptional boy went around to collect spoonfuls of soup for Mendel and ended up with a big bowl just for him. He recovered somewhat.

At the time of liberation Mendel had to be hospitalised. I

could not visit during his hospitalisation and, not having seen him for quite a long time, believed he had died. But eventually we were reunited and left together for France.

The castle of Ambloy, with its 40 rooms, the park and lake at our disposal, appeared truly magnificent, a real paradise. We were very happy for we were allowed to do as we wished. I feel very sorry for myself when I think about what I had to go through during the war, but not about my experiences at Ambloy.

After Passover of 1946, I went to the yeshiva at Aix-Les-Bains where I met a group of boys from Taverny who were waiting to leave for Palestine. Recalling my father's love for the Holy Land, I decided to go there too. I returned to Taverny for a few days to get my brother, but he refused to come along. His plan was to become rich in America and then follow me to Palestine. I returned to my friends and we started off. At the end of a very, very long journey, we arrived safely at the Gur Yeshiva in Jerusalem.

We were warmly received and our arrival was celebrated with a banquet. The Directors of the yeshiva understood that we were unable to handle another separation and allowed us to remain together. They formed a special group at the yeshiva just for us.

The older students helped us catch up on the lessons we had missed. Because I was the youngest and had lost two or three years of studies, the teacher instructed me privately during the evenings.

The Rabbi of Gur did not see me personally, but his spirit shed its light over all of us. We felt fully understood even by those who had not been in Europe during the war. In the beginning, we talked endlessly about the camps, recalling every single detail, every day of life there. Then, little by little, we refrained from mentioning the camps in our conversations.

When I was 21 years old, I met a young Hassidic girl who

was born in Jerusalem. Because of our similar religious convictions and the fact that she was a sweet and gentle girl, I married her. I studied nine more years and became the teacher of the younger children at Gur.

Mendel — The Talmudist

Like his brother Eli, Mendel had no idea what was in store for him in Yavichewitz. He had to work very hard, much too hard for his youth and strength. As a result he suffered from severe pain in his legs and feet.

> I had been given two pairs of pants in the camp. Eli had only one pair that was so large that he had to hold them up with both hands. I exchanged one pair of my pants for a leather belt that I gave to Eli to wrap around his waist and for a wooden spoon that he could use for eating soup.

> My father, who always tried to obtain news about the events outside of the camp, was ridiculed by the other inmates who reminded him that all that counted in the camps was having thick soup. At first, I did not understand what they meant but I quickly became like the others, obsessed with how to get enough to eat. I saw how some men were reduced to animal-like behaviour.

> I was convinced that I would not survive. At the time of liberation, I fell sick with typhus. The Hungarian doctor who treated me tried to convert me to communism and urged me to return to Hungary. Although I was not yet 17, I refused to listen to him. As for the doctor, he did return to Hungary where he was sentenced to 10 years in prison.

> I spent some time in the sanatorium when I first arrived in France and continued to get sick frequently, even in Taverny. Even worse were the terrible nightmares that haunted me every night. I dreamt about a forest, about children who were going to be shot and whom we tried to hide. I used to wake up at night

covered with sweat and when the memories occurred during the day, I felt as if my head would burst.

In Taverny, I only wanted to study the Talmud, but Judith insisted that I learn a trade. I was sent to an electrical shop where I swept the floors and went on errands. I came back after one day and told Judith not to ever send me back there, that I was determined to stay and study. I then decided to try and earn a lot of money and left for Antwerp to become a diamond cutter. When I finished my apprenticeship, a severe economic crisis had developed and I felt I had learned a trade that was not worth anything. So I returned to Taverny and asked an aunt in America to send me an affidavit.

My family in the United States received me warmly and was very understanding. I entered a yeshiva in 1947 and two years later married a young woman I met through my aunt. In 1953, I got a job as an instructor in Cleveland but was later transferred to New York. Tiring of these moves, I finally accepted a post in Israel and settled down permanently.

My wife was also a survivor and we avoided speaking of the camps between ourselves for we feared the return of our nightmares.

But my recurring dream about the children and the forest never left.

I didn't go to a psychiatrist for it because I didn't think I could be helped. I do receive 40 percent disability allowance for my psychiatric problems, but none for physical disability, although my legs and my back hurt as a result of the heavy labour I was forced to perform in the camps.

My wife Rifka, who survived Auschwitz and was liberated at Bergen-Belsen, had joined her brother and sister-in-law in the United States. All of them were camp survivors. When I met her in New York, my having lived through the same ordeals as she did seemed to give her a sense of security. She told me that an American-born woman, used to certain luxuries, would never have accepted living like we did during our first few years of marriage. We lived with our four little children in one room. Fortunately the yeshiva supplied food, for I had no money of my own. It was a hard life but this is what I wanted to do and my wife agreed. Although it became easier for us later on, Rifka continued to sew dresses for our daughters and organise our home.

Our seven children are now happily married. Rifka and I agreed to follow the tradition of choosing their partners and visiting with the parents to arrange the marriage. Our children were allowed to refuse but recognised we were knowledgeable in these matters. After all, how much does a boy whose experience is limited to studying at the yeshiva really know? He trusts his parents to make the proper choice for him. Young people will mature together during the course of their married life.

I am very happy living in Israel. We feel at home here. Traffic stops during Shabbat and people can walk in the streets. This isn't the case in New York, not even in Brooklyn or the Williamsburg neighbourhood where most of the residents are Jewish.

Joshua — The Children's Home Director

Joshua was 16 years old when he arrived in Taverny. He was a gentle and mature boy with an open mind and an interest in Western culture. His tuberculosis required him to spend several months in hospital. I had asked the Israeli scouts to accept him in their boarding home in Southern France, so that he could enjoy the warm climate and use the workshops there.

I met him again in Israel where he had married and raised a family. He was the Director of a Youth Aliyah home for 160 children, which was known to be the best in the country.

His childhood in Lodz, Poland, had been a happy one. His father, a member of the congregation of the Rabbi of Gur, was a businessman more interested in the Talmud than his business. Nevertheless the family was quite well off. When Germany declared war on Poland, they tried to escape to the East, but it was too late. In 1940, the ghetto was already tightly secured.

> I will never forget the conduct of the Polish population. They were spiteful and hateful. They dragged Germans into our apartments and robbed and brutalized the Jews. They hid behind the occupiers and, without receiving orders, unleashed their terrible hatred.
>
> Soon after our arrival in the ghetto, my father fell ill and died on the day of the Jewish New Year in 1940. We were allowed to bury him in the Jewish cemetery of our town.
>
> The head of the Judenrat (Jewish Council), as director of all orphanages in our community, attempted to save the Jewish children. He requisitioned the best section of the ghetto and transferred 1,600 children there, including my little sister and myself. We went to school and had better food than the other inhabitants of the ghetto. To please the head of the Judenrat, who also lived in this section, we practiced military parades during the week and marched past our "Mayor" on Sundays. He was very sickly himself, but he drove out to the public square in his coach and happily watched "his children." As for us, we just loved the rehearsals and the parades.
>
> One morning, accompanied by our supervisors, we were told to assemble in the public square of the large ghetto. Many other Jews, my mother, my older sister and my brothers, among them, were already standing there. Large trucks were lined up and we knew what was going to happen. We were being taken to an extermination camp nearby. Although the square was tightly secured by the ghetto's Jewish policemen, the children slipped through their legs and were able to hide in the cellars. My mother, my brothers, and my older sister were deported that day. You had to cross the entire town to reach the railroad junction and my older sister managed to escape during the

journey and fled to Russia. Only after the war did I discover that she found refuge in Tashkent.

Not a single child remained in the public square that evening and the Germans started their search that night. They found us all, sent us back to the orphanage, and made several head counts. There were 1,600 children. We were loaded onto carts, 20 or 30 at a time, guarded by Jewish policemen, one in the front and another in the back. They told us that if we escaped they would be taken instead so they begged us not to run away. Their fear was an indication that the worst was still to come. For one and a half days we were left in a large empty hospital. The policemen constantly counted us, registering even those who left for the toilets. The supervisors bathed us, trimmed our hair, and pinched our cheeks to make us look healthy and gave us our best clothing to wear. On the way down the staircase I tightly held my little sister's hand. An SS officer stood at the foot of the steps and, seeing our beautiful clothes and healthy looks, made us step to the right. One hundred and seventy-five of us were left standing in the courtyard, alone and unguarded. We didn't know what was going on. Then we heard trucks stopping outside and a lot of noise. Suddenly an SS man opened the door and said that two are missing. Concerned only about the correct count, he haphazardly grabbed two children from the group.

I was 13 1/2 years old then. They brought us back to the ghetto and confined two boys, my little sister and myself in an empty apartment. I don't know why, but an important looking woman in charge of distributing vegetables took a liking to me and made me run errands for her. It gave me the chance to bring home some food in the evenings. Without it, we would have starved to death.

In 1944, it was my turn to be deported. The worst thing is that I was separated from my little sister. I knew that I would never see her again. I was sent to a work camp near Lodz.

Because I was just a young boy, I was given the chore of peeling potatoes in the kitchen. Two of my father's friends were also working there and they took care of me. During our evacuation to Buchenwald, we travelled for two weeks in open railroad cars and I contracted typhus. These two men carried me from the train to the infirmary. If it hadn't been for them I would have died.

I was still in the hospital, lying next to Naphtali at the time of liberation. At first I was very happy to be free but I soon realised that a curtain had been drawn over the past and that nothing would ever bring it back. I fell into deep despair. Many of the other children experienced the same reaction and did not want to live. In their distress, some greedily stuffed themselves with food, swallowing whole pieces of chicken and died.

In France I met members of the Youth Movement Yeshurun who had established their summer camp in Ambloy. Watching these nice, young devoted Jews, laughing and having fun together, I saw a remote chance of someday finding happiness and being able to smile again.

I don't think that I would have been able to lead a normal life right after Buchenwald. The protective atmosphere of Taverny was an indispensable stage of transition. During my psychology studies, I read Erikson and Gesell, who claimed that to become an adult, a child must pass through various stages including childhood and adolescence. If he misses one, he must recapture it later in life. For me, these stages were restored in Taverny.

Later I worked as an instructor at the Scout's home. The headmistress concealed from me an affidavit that an aunt had sent me from the United States. She believed she was doing the right thing in keeping me in France because instructors were needed. However, I was furious about this misuse of power and left the home to work elsewhere as a counsellor, first in Versailles, then in Taverny. At the time I joined Taverny there were only children with social problems in our home, not the Buchenwald child survivors. In 1952, I was sent to yeshiva Kol Torah in Jerusalem and then to a training course where I felt guided by the hand of God because I met Sara. We married two years later. I became Chief Counsellor of the Jewish Boarding School in Paris, studied at the University, and finally became Director of a children's home in Israel in 1956. That is where I live with my wife and our five children.

I make every effort to lead a harmonious family life. That is best for my children and also serves as an example to those living in the home. We follow the example of Taverny, all doors are kept open, and the children may come in any time and observe everything. The girls imitate whatever Sara is doing. Once married, they prepare the same cakes and cut the lemons like she does. They copy their lifestyles from ours.

I do not mention the camps except to other survivors. I went for a long time without being troubled by memories, but I have started having nightmares. I was told that this was absolutely normal. Even after 35 years, a traumatic shock will bear consequences and cause nightmares. I know that this has happened to others. Many of the former deported children had forgotten this period of their life and started suffering disorders much later. I think that the Holocaust must forever remain in people's memories. What bothers me is that during commemorative celebrations for victims of deportation, only the courage of the Warsaw insurgents is highly praised. It is a great error to believe that others only behaved as if sheep being led to the slaughterhouse. The supervisors climbed into our trucks without being asked, in order to stay with us children. Dr. Korczak, the director of the Warsaw orphanage, accompanied his 200 children to Treblinka of his own free will. My father's friends saved my life. Heroic deeds were performed every day in the camps.

ELIE WIESEL

W hy single out one person of 426 for special consideration? We know from the struggles of every one of the children and adolescents (and young adults) who were on the convoy to Écouis, that each deserves special consideration. For have not the vast majority achieved a life of distinction, given such a brutal background of torment and loss? Have not the majority found gainful employment, become loving fathers and loving husbands, contributed to their communities and fought daily against disillusionment and despair?

Perhaps we must say something about Elie Wiesel, precisely because he is only one of 426 persons, in order to appreciate more deeply what was lost. We pay tribute not only to his talents and contributions but also reflect on the meaning of the murders of one and a half million Jewish children. If even only one in 500 children had the potential for extraordinary achievements, the world would have been enriched by 3,000 more intellectual giants.

It is no wonder that one sees in Elie Wiesel a sadness, the sadness of a persistent awareness of the missing. It may indeed be part of every young survivor's life: the silent presence of silenced family and companions of another time.

And what has Elie Wiesel contributed? In a sense, he has rescued religious faith from the ashes of Auschwitz. Had silence prevailed, the slaughter of Europe's Jews would surely have eroded faith like a growing cancer. The Nazi perpetrators and their henchmen, primarily Christians — and the victims, primarily Jewish — neither could have survived the fundamental assault on the religions involved in this tragic encounter.

Wiesel gave voice to what could not be spoken, believed or understood. He struggled to break the silence and thereby inspired theologians to confront the Holocaust and provide an opportunity to re-examine the basic tenets of their

Elie Wiesel (Photo by Robert Mordechai Edel)

faith. In a post-Holocaust world he surely expanded humanity's encounter with G-D and deepened faith and commitment.

Elie's insatiable intellectual curiosity was in evidence at Ambloy where he was a close friend of Daniel's, who became a famous physicist. Elie mastered French within one year and after completing his studies, became the Paris correspondent for an Israeli newspaper. In his tiny apartment he worked for the newspaper and continued the study of Talmud with Mr. Shushani.

It was at Ambloy where Elie Wiesel wrote his first memories in a notebook in Yiddish. It was the original version of what was to become his book "Night."

Eight hundred pages long, it was first published in Yiddish in Buenos Aires, Argentina titled, "Und Die Welt Hot Geschwiegen" (And the World Remained Silent) in 1956.

During the 1950s, the French President, Pierre Mendès-France, was a popular figure, particularly after successfully ending the war in Indochina. The Israeli newspaper sought an interview with him, but he never granted interviews during his term in office. Elie instead approached François Mauriac, a fervent defender of the French President during his battles with critics and political enemies. Mauriac, a writer, agreed to see the young reporter.

François Mauriac's intellectual curiosity connected with the sympathy he felt for Wiesel, adding a personal dimension to their first conversation. The tragic experiences of the young man made a deep impression on Mauriac, but those experiences were connected by him to themes in Catholic spiritual life, such as suffering, forgiveness and redemption. This was too much for Elie who stood up to leave but was held back by Mauriac. Elie explained to him that he could not accept that the ordeals he had endured and which led to the murder of millions would be reduced to a divine mystery with moral implications. François Mauriac listened to him, asked questions, and encouraged him to inform the general public of his experiences. In short, he encouraged him to write a book, which appeared in 1958, as "Night" with a foreword by Mauriac.

They remained friends and when Elie Wiesel was awarded the Prix Médicis honoring the best foreign author writing in French, the illustrious old man came to congratulate the younger man he considered a younger brother.

In the late 1950's Elie went to New York with no particular intention to settle there but he was hit by a taxi and seriously injured. During his long hospitalization and recovery, his French visa expired and he remained in the United States.

As a writer, journalist, lecturer and professor, his influence grew widely. His works encompassed the complexity of Jewish destiny, strongly informed by his Hassidic background. He is deeply concerned about the fate of his people and is their champion everywhere, whether in Israel, the former USSR, or at the United Nations. His influential book "Jews of Silence" helped breach the Iron Curtain, which eventually led to the immigration of hundreds of thousands of Russian Jews to the free world. On awarding him a prize, then President of Israel

Yitzhak Navon stated that Elie's travels take him around the globe and that his address is the universe.

Elie Wiesel's concerns are not only for his Jewish brethren. They extend to the oppressed, no matter where. He has been personally involved in American civil rights, in the fight against oppression in Latin America, in combating hunger in Cambodia, and drawing attention to the slaughters in Bosnia. Wherever he feels he can make a difference, he appears in order to plead for an end to indifference, for people to become involved and help to combat evil.

In 1986 he was awarded the Nobel Peace Prize. Elie Wiesel's activism has led to special relationships with American presidents and world leaders. President Jimmy Carter invited him to head the US Holocaust Memorial Council which eventually led to the establishment of the US Holocaust Memorial Museum in Washington, DC.

In a conversation with one of us (J.H.) he said,

> Our persecution must never be forgotten. I have taken it upon myself to keep it in everyone's memory. Yet although I mention the camps during my lectures, I cannot describe what happened there. For many years I could not utter the word 'Auschwitz.' I teach 'Knowledge of Humanity' at Boston University where more students sign up than there are places in my class. I always accept the children of my friends from Taverny, those who themselves are unable to speak of their past and therefore send them to me as students. I tell them about Hassidism and what the holy communities accomplished before being consumed by flames. The world was not worthy of their existence.
>
> I watched the movie 'Holocaust' on television. It was an insult to those of us who were there, for the reality of life in the concentration camps was falsified and distorted. It disturbs me deeply for I introduced the term 'Holocaust' in my writings. I am not pleased at all with that word and yet it has become adopted worldwide. The meaning of Holocaust is, in fact, consensual

sacrifice, whereas we speak of a catastrophe (Shoah). A more precise term is genocide.

I married late in life. For a long time I hesitated to bring a child into this world, a world about which I feel so pessimistic. Today, my child is my most precious possession. Watching him grow up reminded me of my relationship with my father. He spoke very little and I had to guess at his feelings and intentions. I talk a lot with my son and take him with me on my travels. He has received a traditional education at a Jewish school.

Elie Wiesel emphasizes that what he does, he does as a Jew. He writes, behaves and leads with a keen awareness of his origins. With the strength derived from his Jewish identity and his Jewish experience, he is able to understand with compassion the tragedies and plight of others.

It is because all of us are in debt to him for assisting in our own struggle with faith, depression, hope, despair, pessimism, issues of life and death, grief and loss, that we pay particular attention to this survivor, one of the children of Buchenwald.

George Goldbloom at 1995 Reunion — 50th Anniversary of liberation

Elie Wiesel at 1995 Reunion

Joseph Dziubak, George Goldbloom, Jerry Kappelus

Merna and Jerry Kappelus

OBSERVATIONS AND CONCLUSION

*F*our hundred and twenty-six children, adolescents and youths — the remnants — their bonds forged from having experienced unparalleled suffering and grievous losses.

For them, Taverny was an interlude, a moment in time to recapture the fragments necessary to rebuild a meaningful existence. Their lives before the war, so cruelly interrupted, required reconnecting to the post-war present in order to be able to look to the future. Except for those too young even to have pre-war memories.

Was it the adaptation to a "normal" life that presented the problem? Elie Wiesel writes, "The truth is, it was not that difficult — less difficult than adjusting to death. Having slept with the dead and spent a lifetime — indeed, many lifetimes — in death's company, we had come to view it as ordinary, expected, a daily presence, the norm, not the exception. We had, after all, been brought to the camp not to live, but to die, and when we stumbled over a corpse, we walked on without so much as a second look."[1]

This dynamic figured prominently in the episode of concern where Judith worried that someone had fallen under a train. The boys could not imagine that anyone cared whether they lived. They were accustomed to no one caring about their deaths. Death was commonplace in their lives.

It is important to note that the children of Taverny were those who opted for a traditional, religious life, including the wish for kosher food. The accounts in this book therefore represent mostly the children and adolescents who in adult

---

1. Elie Wiesel. *Memoirs: All Rivers Run to the Sea.* New York: Alfred A. Knopf, 1995.

life remained very concerned about the religious upbringing of their own children as orthodox Jews.

Nearly all 426 boys came from strictly orthodox homes, but the faith of many had been sorely tried and they no longer believed in G-D or held ambivalent attitudes towards religious observance.

The lifelong journeys after April 11, 1945, reveal an enormous variety in paths chosen career-wise, in marriage and in observance. Notwithstanding the dispersion to all corners of the globe, the boys from Buchenwald remain devoted to one another to this day, as if part of a large extended family.

There is much to learn from each life story of devastation and recovery. We pick only a few themes of special interest.

Brothers

Throughout the accounts we find reference to brothers surviving together: David and Abraham (with cousin Moshe), Lulek and Naphtali, Meyer and Daniel, Eli and Mendel.

What is striking about brothers surviving together is how often the younger one provided the strength for the older to continue the struggle. Some older brothers were described by the younger as less decisive, more preoccupied and reflective. Could it be that the older ones could see the hopelessness of their situation? Were the younger ones less conceptually able to do that and therefore more focussed on day-to-day survival? Were they perhaps proud as youngsters to be needed by the older brothers? It could have been that the older brothers were worked harder and beaten more often, perhaps leading to a greater state of weakness even than the younger ones. Whatever the precise circumstances, the younger ones served at times as a source of inspiration.

And yet, later in life, it is not infrequently the younger sibling who appears less secure, less decisive, more ambivalent about relationships and sometimes unmarried.

Had they peaked too early in life, grown old too soon, too quickly? Did they revert just as quickly back into a childhood that had been lost? Was it the absence of parental guidance never received which accounts for their late life uncertainty and insecurity?

Even where the older brother remained in charge and stronger, part of that strength derived from the commitment to save the younger.

Naphtali had torn seven year-old Lulek from their mother's arms as she was taken away. Some time later in the camps Lulek described Naphtali near war's end as a "Mussulman." Naphtali had reached the stage of the living dead. In Michel's narrative he states that Lulek saved his brother's life a few days before liberation by hiding him in "our barracks." Yet soon after liberation, Naphtali again assumes responsibility for his younger brother's welfare, including his travel to Palestine and placement with family.

In Eli's narrative, he describes himself as so weak that his older brother Mendel carried him most of the way on the death march to Buchenwald. Despite the life-saving closeness, Eli wanted to go to Palestine and Mendel to America. After liberation, Mendel suffered from terrible nightmares. He married in America a survivor of Auschwitz and Bergen-Belsen. They did not talk of their experiences for fear of triggering more memories and nightmares. However, the younger brother Eli married a native-born Israeli.

Marriages

The eventual in-laws of both Romek and Lulek feared for the well being of their daughters married to the survivors of atrocities. After all, how much damage had been done? Could one have a normal relationship after such massive trauma? It is likely that they themselves had doubts.

During the recovery at Taverny, the boys fell in love with their directors. Kalman was determined to marry Niny and remained single his entire life. Katsef named his beloved cow Judith, and later married a non-Jew.

The boys at Taverny fantasized about romance, while their traditional, observant upbringing guided their actual behaviour. Rabbi Meyer-Tzvi could not go to America and face his congregation unmarried, so he became engaged to the picture of his intended before meeting and marrying her in the United States.

Earlier we alluded to the possibility that those who acknowledged the deaths of their parents and said Kaddish for them were able to begin mourning and were likely to marry women of non-survivor background. Those who refused to give up hope and who postponed their grief and bereavement were more likely to marry other survivors. What can we make of this? Was it not possible to defy reality and maintain a faint hope with a non-survivor partner? Did the person in an effort to stave off the inevitable, feel more comfort with a person who lived in similar denial? Or in similar hope?

Neither situation guaranteed a greater comfort with respect to silence. A survivor married to a non-survivor was not likely to speak of the past and disturb her with his visions, and if one married another survivor, why speak of it? It was known to both and neither wished to trigger the other's memories and nightmares.

Shalom Robinson and Judith Hemmendinger re-interviewed 14 persons in Israel and France who had been members of the child survivors of Buchenwald.[1] Of eight who emigrated to Israel and had married, only one was divorced. Six held white-collar jobs as a government official, a rabbi, children's home director, an office worker, schoolteacher, and two others held blue-collar jobs.

Of six persons in France, all were married and working.

Anger, Rage and Hatred

In many accounts, continuing hatred was expressed towards Germans (mostly confined only to the generation which included the perpetrators), towards Hungarians, Poles and other nationalities (usually those who were virulently anti-Semitic as were the Hungarian Nazis). Some survivors avoid setting foot in Germany, others refuse to purchase German-made products and others do not provide services to those who remind them of their persecutors.

The first observers to see the children described them as "a homogenous mass, with no hair, faces swollen from hunger and uniform clothes: a group with an apathetic, unconcerned and indifferent attitude, with no laughter or even a smile, and a marked aggressiveness towards the personnel; mistrust and suspicion."[2]

---

1. Shalom Robinson and Judith Hemmendinger. Psychosocial adjustment 30 years later of people who were in Nazi concentration camps as children. Stress and Anxiety Vol. 8 (Eds. Charles D. Spielberger and Irwin G. Sarason. Guest Editor Norman Milgram) Washington: Hemisphere, 1982.
2. Judith Hemmendinger: A la sortie des camps de la mort: Réinsertion dans la vie (Coming out of the death camps: Return to life). Israel Journal of Psychiatry 18(4):331-334, 1981.

And this was after a period of recovery! From April 11 to June 8, 1945 these children remained in Buchenwald. Upon arrival in Écouis in mid-June, their first stop in France, they were better fed and better dressed but angry and enraged. Who could blame them? Whatever their national origin, most of them had been persecuted, starved and beaten for as long as six years. During that time, the least sign of physical resistance or anger towards the enemy resulted in instant death. Where did the anger go? Is the reader surprised to hear that it may have lasted a lifetime? Some anger was vented at Écouis, often towards the directors and to each other. What is actually remarkable is the fact that there is no known instance of revenge on part of this particular group of young survivors. They did not kill their captors even when they had regained some strength or were offered the opportunity.

Rage is not much discussed by students of the medical and psychological literature on Holocaust survivors.[1] One problem has been that it was often avoided by therapists and not understood by the naïve well meaning people who preached forgiveness without having endured the experience. Adolf Gawalewicz[2] arrived from Auschwitz to Sweden and was asked philosophic questions about the "human condition" based on his experiences by a refined Swedish lady. His response, "But let us theoretically make a small experiment; let us crowd 100 people such as you or even better ones — if they exist at all — in a cattle wagon for eight days without giving them anything to eat and not even a drop to drink, I repeat, not a drop. On the ninth day we may organize with those who came out alive from those wagons the discussion of the subject of people who are naturally good. Those persons will already be at least partly prepared for such a discussion." Where did the rage go? It did not go away. It stayed. Clinicians have suggested that it led inwardly to depression and guilt feelings. Perhaps. But the chronic grief and loss are quite enough to account for depression and depressive memories. And guilt belongs to those who

---

1. See Robert Krell. The psychiatric treatment of Holocaust survivors In: Charny, Israel W. (Ed.) The Widening Circle of Genocide. Genocide: A Critical Bibliographic Review: Vol. 3 New Brunswick, New Jersey: Transaction, pp. 245-271; and Robert Krell. Alternative therapeutic approaches to Holocaust survivors In: Marcus, Paul, and Rosenberg, Alan (Eds.), Healing Their Wounds: Psychotherapy with Holocaust Survivors and Their Families. New York: Praeger, 1989, pp. 215-226.
2. Adolph Gawalewicz. A number gets back its name. In: Auschwitz Anthology. Vol. 3: It Did Not End in Forty-Five. Part 1. Warsaw: International Auschwitz Committee, 1971, pp. 29-31.

committed acts for which they should feel guilt. The guilt experienced by those who could not do more for a family member or fellow inmate because of the hideous circumstances that made intervention impossible, that is different.

We believe the anger persists and can be reactivated by any of a thousand reminders, day or night. Often the rage is simply too great for words and the survivor lapses into silence. What is remarkable is that so many of these Buchenwald boys have begun to tell their stories, to bear witness, and to do so particularly for adolescents in high school, the age at which they themselves were in slave labour camps, Auschwitz and Buchenwald. It is a constructive response to a potentially self-destructive anger.

The Children of Survivors

A disconcerting theme throughout these accounts is the maintaining of silence within families. Rabbi Moshe had not mentioned his experiences to his children yet expresses the feeling that Auschwitz as a symbol of the Holocaust must never be forgotten.

Rabbi Meyer-Tzvi, who had become engaged to an unknown cousin languishing in a displaced persons camp, prior to his departure to the United States, noted that he never talked with his children but did write down his memories for them.

Simon's son insisted on being present at the interview with his father for he wanted to know what his father had experienced. To that time he had not been told.

Michel took his sons to Yad Vashem in 1983.

We do not know if the sharing of their past was a function of the age of their children or the stage of life of the parent.

By the time of the first reunion in 1965, those with families had children still too young to be told of their father's experiences. But later?

Rabbi Lau's 1984 account reveals that he too said little about himself even while speaking publicly at commemorations. Robert Waisman successfully kept his past to himself until 1983 when he became aware of the existence of Holocaust denial. Perhaps it took until the 1980s, a time span of 40 years, for anyone to feel secure enough in the ordinary pursuits of a normal life to be able to speak about the war. And who can fault them for withholding information which remains part of personal nightmares to this day and which the parents surely did not want to instill into the dreams of their children?

The problem, the tension, lay always in the fact that even without words, survivor's children were surrounded by mystifying cues which worried them. Perhaps also, they perceived or even received some of the anger or rage in the parent.

Over 50 years of medical and psychological literature[1] reveals numerous opinions and research conclusions conducted with the children of survivors. Some research supports the notion that children of survivors have no more problems than a similar age cohort. Other studies on children of survivors support the concept that psychologic damage was inflicted by survivor parents. Unwarranted generalizations have been made about Holocaust survivors who were required to submit to psychiatric examinations for restitution claims and had to demonstrate psychopathology. Other generalisations were drawn from the children of Holocaust survivors who were brought to psychiatric clinics.

These complex issues are not our immediate concern here. What is troubling is that there may be adult children of survivors who still do not know their parents' life experiences, nor do they know much about their pre-war families. It is a potential shadow over one's existence not to know the circumstances of one's origins and family identity. A number of survivors have tenaciously withheld information, meaning to protect their children from knowing and to save them unnecessary suffering and worry. What may have been a wise decision when their children were young has become counterproductive. There is a need for children and grandchildren to know in order to reduce their fantasies (sometimes as traumatic as reality), to demystify certain misunderstood family communications such as when survivors misidentify a child using the name of a lost relative, and commemorative rituals which may seem strange when the stimulus remains a mystery. What is a child to make of a father who begins every day lighting a memorial candle in his basement?

---

1. Robert Krell and Marc Sherman (Eds.) Medical and psychological effects of concentration camps on Holocaust survivors. In: Vol. 4 Genocide: A Critical Bibliographic Review. New Brunswick (USA) and London (UK): Transaction, 1997.

The children of survivors have been in the uncomfortable position of not understanding their parents' occasional sadness and tears on otherwise happy occasions, or have witnessed unexpected outpourings of grief without explanation. Without clarification, a child was likely to think they were the cause of that grief.

Despite their profoundly troubled beginnings, Holocaust survivors have managed to raise children well enough that the larger epidemiological studies reveal no discernable differences between them and the general population. In

Group of 1995 Reunion

Back Row:1. Mark Korzuch (Argentina) 2. Unidentified
3. Henry Dymant (Paris) 4. Robbie Waisman (Vancouver)
Second Row: 5. Jacque Finkelstein (Paris) 6. George Goldbloom (Miami)
7. Willy Fogel (Paris) 8. Unidentified 9.Unidentified David Perlmutter.
Third Row: 11. Arie Rosemberg (NY), Jerry Kapelus (Toronto)
Joe Oziobak (Miami) 14. Simon Michalowicz (Australia) 15. Chaim Finkelstein.

fact, while there are children of survivors who may have suffered from their Holocaust legacy, there are also children of survivors who have been inspired by that same legacy to do good and decent things.

In fact, there is some indication that children of survivors are over-represented numerically in the helping professions, such as nursing, psychology and psychiatry.

Of the 426 survivors on the original convoy list, the majority have married, worked and raised families. Those we know personally to this day, are proud and committed parents. Who could have thought on April 11, 1945, that any child of that barely living remnant, representing so many murdered children, would succeed against such overwhelming odds to live a productive and meaningful life? Not the experts.

APPENDIX
THE CONVOY LIST

ORPHAN CHILDREN FROM BUCHENWALD NOW IN PARIS

ENFANTS VENUS D'ALLEMAGNE — CONVOI DU 8 JUIN 1945.
A ECOUIS (Eure)

Paris List N° 1162 A.

N°	Noms	Prénoms	Date de Naissance	Lieu de Naissance	Pays	Observations
1	ABISCH	Hermann	15/5/29	Felsoviso	Roum.	
2	ABRAMZON	Cejmech	7/5/24	Sulejow	Pol.	
3	ABRAMZON	Abram	23/3/29	Przeburz	"	
4	ABRAMOVICZ	Zysio	30/I/29	Pabianice	"	
5	AJZENBERG	Nuchym	24/4/27	Brody	"	
6	AMSZCZONOWSKI	Jankiel	12/4/28	Lowicz	"	
7	APFELDORFER	Sender	25/II/26	Bereznrlk	Hong.	
8	ARON	Joseph	15/I/30	Cluj	Roum.	
9	ASZTALOS	Joseph	27/8/23	Izaszacsal	"	
IO	AUERHANH	Mozès	14/2/27	Rzeskow	Pol.	
11	AVNER	Srmul	12/3/29	Lodz	"	
I2	HALTER	Elias	2/I/28	Kielce	"	
I3	BAUL	Szyla	21/5/26	Ostrowiec	"	
I4	BAUM	Pincus	30/6/28	Polica	"	
I5	BECKER	Izsak	19/9/28	Wadowitz	"	
I6	BERGUT VEL REICHER Zelig		27/I2/28	Krakow	"	
I7	BIRNBAUM	Aron	24/I2/28	Sosnowiec	"	
I8	BLAUSTEIN	Josef	4/9/28	Legesbenye	Hong.	
I9	BRULL	Simon	26/7/25	Mozokovacshaza	"	
20	BULWA	Aron	27/I2/29	Piotrkow	Pol.	
2I	BURGMAN	Szulim	14/I/28	Czestochawa	"	
22	BUZYN	Léon	7/I/29	Lodz	"	
23	CHARMACZ	Fiszel	10/12/28	Kielce	"	
24	CIMENT	Lipot	10/I/30	Szatmarnemeti	Roum/
25	CZITROM	Laszlo	2/4/3I	Nagyvarad	"	
26	CODIKOW	Chaskiel	9/4/30	Kovno	Lith.	
27	CYNAMON	Leib	7/9/28	Buzeziny	Pol.	
28	CYROWSKI	Reuben	7/ /29	Pabianice	"	
29	CYMBERKNOPF	Jakub	2/7/20	Sosznowiec	"	
30	"	Nathan	II/II/27	"	"	
3I	CZAPNIK	Abram	30/II/30	Lodz	"	
32	CZARNY	Lebusz	4/8/28	Cznstochowa	"	
33	DAZKAL	Jakub	25/2/28	Dragomeret	Roum.	
34	DAWIDOWITSCH	Meuder	12/I2/28	Marmorosch	"	
35	DEITELBAUM	Rudolf	27/6/28	Reghin	"	
36	DEUTSCH	Otto	II/8/28	Babein	" "	
37	DEUTSCH	Erwin	19/8/27	"	"	
38	"	Moritz	24/4/28	Radziejow	Pol.	
39	DICKERMANN	Michael	2/2/27		"	
40	DIENER	Pal	12 /I/28	Szalmarnemetz	Roum.	
4I	DORMENBERG	David	17/5/29	Halmen	"	
42	DOTSCH	Gabor	23/2/29		Hongr.	
43	DYMANT	Abram	2 6/3/17	Kozienoc	Pol.	
44	DYMANT	Chaim	30/IO/19	"	"	
45	DYMANT	Herszek	31/IO/28	"	"	
46	DYMENTZSTAJN	Joachim	5/3/28	Sosnowiec	"	
47	DZILBAK	Joseph	14/8/29	Lodz	"	
48	ELLENBOGEN	Zoltan	18/4/28	Nyirbator	Hongr.	

- 2 -

ORPHAN CHILDREN FROM BUCHENWALD NOW IN PARIS

ENFANTS VENUS D'ALLEMAGNE - CONVOI DU 8 JUIN 1945
A ECOUIS (Eure)

Paris List N° 1162 .

49	ENGLANDER	Matton	II/II/28	Szatmar	Hongr.
50	ERNST	Miklos	19/5/29	Typest	"
5I	FACHLER	Joseph	6/2/29	Bodzetyr	Pol.
52	FARKAS	Chaim	3/8/28	Borsa	Roum.
53	FARKAS	Erwin	5/6/3I	Oradéa	"
54	FARKAS	Mendel	I0/I/28	Karynosavj	"
55	FARKOWTZ	Martin	8/5/23		"
56	FEIG	Lamar	5/5/29	Visent	"
57	FEIN	Idel	I/I/30	Kowno	Lith.
58	FELD	Chrsz	18/I/28	Krakow	Pol.
59	FELDBERG	Aron	I5/4/28	Bedzin	"
60	FEUERBERG	Abraham	I5/I/28	Bacau	Hongr.
6I	FINKERLSTEIN-Salek		9/7/3I	Movikarczyn	Pol.
62	FINKERLSTAJN-Chaim		I3/8/29	Strsemioszyce	"
63	"	Jakob	I/2/32	"	"
64	FISCHMAN	Zoltan	4/6/28	Kaletele	Roum.
65	"	Hersch	I/5/28	Sighet	"
66	FISCHMAN	Mendel	22/3/29	"	"
67	FLUGELMANN	Abraham	II/7/23	Opatiew	Pol.
38	FOGEL	Perec	23/8/23	Ronadejos	Roum.
69	FOGEL	Izsak	4/4/29	"	"
70	FOGEL	Jeno	8/5/28	Satmar	"
7I	FOJGEL	Wolf	I5/8/28	Dziatoszuce	Pol.
72	FREILICH	Moritz	25/I0/28	Pjotskow	"
73	FREIMAN	Mozek	29/9/28	Chorzáb	"
74	FRENKEL	Samuel	I2/3/27		Tché.
75	FRIEDMAN	Herman	5/5/29	Rachow	
76	FRIEDMAN	Leb	28/5/29	Viseul de Sus	Roum.
77	FROM	Natan	I7/7/27	Sosnowiec	Pol.
78	FROMAN	Zysman	8/II/29	Bedzin	"
79	FRUCHTER	Zalel	24/4/29	Féliste	Roum.
80	FRUCHTER	Major	6/I0/29	Creesunest	Pol.
8I	FRYDMAN	Léon	30/I2/30	Lodz	Pol.
82	FUCHS	Mor	20/I/28	Oradéa	Roum.
83	FULOP	Marton	2/2/29	Ilenda	"
84	FULOP	Simon	I9/9/28	"	"
85	FUSYNSKI	Abram	27/9/29		Pol.
86	FULOP	Abraham	7/4/28	Surduc	Roum.
87	GANC	Chaim	26/I/29	Maramosos	"
88	GEMUTH	Sandor	24/8/29	Viseul de Sus	"
89	GERSON	Gerszon	I/I/29	Kasimiers	Pol.
90	GERTRUCZ	Mozès	I5/4/28		"
9I	GLIKSMAN	Moniek	I5/I0/29	Pabianice	"
92	GLUCK	Jakob	I5/3/30	Viseul de Sus	Roum.
93	GLUCK	Miklos	2/5/23	Tarkal	Hongr.
94	GODINGER Rafael		25/6/29	Lopusno	Tché.
95	GOLDBERG	Berek	8/II/34	Lodz	Pol.
96	GOLDBERG	Abram	I5/3/23	Zdunska-Wola	"
97	GOLDBLUM	Idel	9/8/29	Lodz	"
98	GOLBERGER	Lipot	4/I0/29	Barochovo	Tché.

- 3 -

ORPHAN CHILDREN FROM BUCHENWALD NOW IN PARIS

ENFANTS VENUS D'ALLEMAGNE - CONVOI DU 8 JUIN 1945.
À ECOUIS (Eure)

Paris List N° 1162 À.

99	GOLDFRAJND	Abram	6/4/30	Sosnowiec	Pol.
100	GOLDFINGER	Marek	30/6/29	Cracovie	"
101	GOLDKRANC	Jochan	5/8/26	Lodz	"
102	GOLDMANN	Idek	5/6/29	Lodz	"
103	GOLDRING	Leib	26/5/29		"
104	GORLICKI	Chil	25/5/28	Chmelnik	Pol.
105	GOTTESMANN	Hermann	12/1/28	Svalawa	Tché.
106	GOTTLIEB	Samuel	12/7/28	Kortow	Pol.
107	GRADEL	Mozek	10/10/25		"
108	GRAMAN	Szaja	7/11/28	Kroí-Huta	"
109	GROJSMAN	Israel	5/5/28	Kanow	"
110	GROSSMANN	Hermann	12/12/31	Slatilskedoly	Tché.
111	GROSSMANN	Laszlo	12/1/28		Hongr.
112	GROSZ	Tibor	24/7/28	Erdöd	Roum.
113	GRUBNER	Rubin	20/10/27	Oswiecin	Pol.
114	GRUNBERG	Lejzor	5/6/28	Kopszywnnica	"
115	GRUNBERG	Uszer	5/6/28	"	"
116	GRUNBERGER	Bela	2/1/28	Valea lui Mihai	Roum.
117	GRUNBERGER	David	22/12/28	Magydarony	"
118	GRUNBERGER	Ludwig	15/7/28	Kurima	Tchéc.
119	GRUNSTEIN	Moniel	5/7/30	Lodz	Pol.
120	GURCIEL	Benjamin	10/7/28	Chmieldnik	"
121	GUTMAN	Stephan	25/4/28	Karolyimani	Roum.
122	HABERFELD	Josef	27/3/26		Hongr.
123	HALBERSTAN	Chaim	20/5/28	Rzeszow	Pol.
124	HANSZ	Szalmon	20/5/29	Krecinest	Tché.
125	HANSZ	Jemay	20/11/28	"	"
126	HAUPTSCHEIN	Pinkus	6/9/27	Oswiecil	Pol.
127	GILBART	Leiser	26/5/29		
128	HERSCHKOWITZ-Salomon		15/3/29	Neresnice	Tché.
129	HERSCHTIG	Salomon	1/3/28	Moisin	Roum.
130	HERSKOWITZ	David	4/9/28	Iléonda	"
131	HERSKOWITZ	Ludwig	6/4/28	Vonyikova	Tché.
132	HERSKOWITZ	Mendel	25/3/28		Pol.
133	HERSZLIKOWICZ-David		15/7/28	Wodsilaw	"
134	HERZEG	Otto	10/12/28	Nishonz	Hongr.
135	HIRSCH	Imre	11/3/28	Szatmarnemetz	Roum.
136	HOCHBERG	Kuba	15/10/28	Lodz	Pol.
137	HOFFMANN	Blek	21/1/31	Sotmarmeti	Roum.
138	HOLLANDER	Abram	1/6/27	Osviecim	Pol.
139	HOROWITZ	Arthur	20/4/28	Marghita	Roum/
140	HOFFMANN	Oszkar	16/8/29	Sighet	"
141	HUTTER	Marton	28/8/29	Nagyorad	"
142	HUSZ	Abram	2/1/29		Tché.
143	IAKOBOWITZ	Samuel	2/10/28	Szigot	"
144	IZSAK	Abraham	29/1/28	Iapa	"
145	JAKAB	Imre	10/2/28		Pol.
146	JAKABOWITZ	Moritz	12/12/29	Jvaczko	Roum.
147	JAKABOWITZ	Sandor	2/4/29	Taavesti	"

- 4 -

ORPHAN CHILDREN FROM BUCHENWALD NOW IN PARIS

ENFANTS VENUS D'ALLEMAGNE - CONVOI DU 8 JUIN 1945
à ECOUIS (Eure)

Paris List N° 1162 A.

148	JAKUBOWICZ	David	12/6/28		Pol.
149	JAKUBOWICZ	Kendel	10/4/26	Piotrkow	"
150	JANOWSKI	Rachmil	11/1/23	Ldmusa	"
151	JEGER	Berko	7/6/28	Rona de Sus	Roum/
152	JEGER	Dezso	28/12/28	Saluta	"
153	JELINOWIECZ	Abram	24/12/29	Pabianice	Pol.
154	JNDIG	Jonas	8/9/28	Dese	Roum.
155	JUDKOVITS	Alek	8/6/28	Oradéa	"
156	JUNGER	Tobias	27/10/28	Carei Marci	"
157	JUROWITZ	Georg	26/5/28	Oroswardon	"
158	KAEZMAREK	Léo	1/1/29	Bydgoszer	Pol.
159	KAHAN	Jeno	16/5/28	Ermihalyfalwa	Roum.
160	ISKOVITS	Henrich	9/4/28	Botiz	Roum.
161	KAHAN	Hermann	10/10/29	Viseul de Sus	"
162	KALIKSZTAJN	Kalman	4/1/28	Strzemieszyce	Pol.
163	KALIKSZTAJN	Heniek	9/6/31	"	"
164	KAMINSKI	Abel	13/4/28	"	"
165	KAPELUSZ	Jakob	30/5/29	Lodz	"
166	KALLUS	Ludwig	13/6/29	Sulestova	Tché.
167	KAMINSKI	Kovla	23/4/26	Bendszin	Pol.
168	KAMINSKI	Aron	19/10/28	Strzemieszyce	"
169	KANE	Fajwen	12/12/28	Tlook	
170	KASSIERER	Bela	3/5/28	Szalika	Tché.
171	KASZOWITZ	Pal	3/5/28	Nagykaroly	Roum.
172	KATZ	Andor	15/9/29	Monkacevo	Tché.
173	KAUFMAN	Mojzesz	17/11/30	Lijet	Roum.
174	KAZANOWSKI	Chaim	1/5/29		Pol.
175	KESTEMBERG	Jehuda	8/4/29	Warschau	Pol.
176	KILSZTOK	Mayer	2/12/28	Bendzin	"
177	KINSTLICHT	Josef	27/9/28		"
KLAJUZAIER		Fajwel	15/9/28	Nowyager	"
179	KLAJAM	Szymon	21/6/28	Praszka	"
180	KLAJMAN	Gerszon	6/6/28	Nowy-Ljcz	"
181	KLAJNCRENDLER-Idek		8/1/32	Sucha	"
182	KLAJNER	Mozek	16/10/29		"
183	KLEIN	Majer	1/5/29	Uschorod	Tché.
184	KLEIN	Mano	7/4/28	Islava	"
185	KLEIN	MARKUS	6/8/28	Bekenyova	"
186	KLEIN	Dezider	15/12/28	Satoralzaribyhely	"
187	KLEIN	Jéramias	29/3/28	Lukazewo	"
188	KLEIN	Sandor	11/7/28	Satmar	Roum.
189	KLEIN	Arnold	21/4/28		"
190	KLEIN	Deszo	3/5/30		"
191	KLEIN	Sandor	12/2/29	Nyrbator	Hongr.
192	KLEIN	Gerso	19/9/28	"	
193	KLEIN	Lazlo	15/1/29	Groswarden	Roum.
194	KLEINMAN	Moritz	22/2/29	Satmar	"
195	KLIGER	Lajb	26/12/28	Lublin	Pol.
196	KLUJMANN	Nachmann	9/6/28		"

- 5 -

ORPHAN CHILDREN FROM BUCHENWALD NOW IN PARIS

ENFANTS VENUS D'ALLEMAGNE - CONVOI DU 8 JUIN 1945
À ECOUIS (Eure)

Paris List N° II62 A.

	HENLOCK				
197	KOCHAN	Henieck	22/3/30	Bendzin	Pol.
198	KOCHAN	Sala	15/3/28	"	"
199	KOHAN	Jona	10/7/29	Felsoiselist	Roum.
200	KOHN	Zoltan	5/6/29	Busting	Tché.
201	KORZENBLATT	Abraham	7/5/31		Pol.
202	KORZUCH	David	6/1/30	Kielce	"
203	KOVAES	Imre	25/3/29	Szalard	Roum/
204	KARPUSINSKI	Israel	25/1/27		
205	KOZUCH	Max	2/3/29	Strzemienyce	Pol.
206	KRAUS	Herman	8/1/30	Uzhorod	Tché.
207	KROUS	Jewo	11/7/31	Miskols-Borzod	Hongr.
208	KUCHARSKI	David	2/12/28	Bendzin	Pol.
209	KULITZ	Moses	7/12/28	Szlakina	Tché.
210	KRAKAUER	Arnold	1/8/39	Chrzanow	Pol.
211	KYBA	Chaim	28/12/28		"
212	LAJTENBERG	Keyt	2/12/25		"
213	LANDAU	Naftali	6/3/28	Banssyhulyad	Roum.
214	LANDAU	Bejniez	6/8/28	Bezesko	Pol.
215	LASZLO	Janos	30/10/28	Oradéa	Roum.
216	LAU	Israel	1/6/37	Piotrkow	Pol.
217	LAU	Naftali	23/6/28	Krakow	"
218	LAUFER	Nathan	18/6/29	Leczyca	"
219	LAZAROWITS	Jakob	10/10/30	Talosremék	Roum.
220	LAZAROWITS	Juda	18/3/29	"	"
221	LEBEWITZ	Frigjes	23/6/28		"
222	LEBOVITZ	Ignac	9/12/28	Szalmar	"
223	LEBOVITZ	Beni	23/8/28	Slatinsko	Tché.
224	LEMPERT	Claudislaus	31/7/28	Oradéa	Roum/
225	LENDER	Jakob	25/9/29	Viseul de Sus	Roum.
226	LENDER	Josef	4/8/28	"	"
227	LERNER	Salomon	9/10/29	Sighet	"
228	LERNER	Chaim	8/5/30	Felsaviso	Hongr;
229	LERNER	Alex	10/12/28	Slatynskie	Tché.
230	LEHRER	Abraham	14/9/27		Pol.
231	LESWZYK	Jakob	10/12/28	Wichau	"
232	LEVENZ	Tibor	8/11/29	Lzirlugos	Hongr.
233	LEWIN	Manfred	27/9/39		Allem.
234	LEWKOWITZ	Léon	20/6/30		Pol.
235	LIBLICH	Szyja	22/3/28	Krakowie	"
236	LICHTENSTEIN	Arthur	1/1/29		Roum.
237	LINER	Horsch	30/3/28	Bialisstock	Pol.
238	LIPSITZ	Bernard	5/2/29	Satoralzaribyhely	Hongr?
239	LIPSITZ	Mozès	18/7/29	Bilke	Tché.
240	LISKER	Henrik	12/2/28	Berlin	Allem.
241	LONDER	Fishchel	16/5/28	Szokonowiec	Pol.
242	LOWINCZ	Imre	5/10/28	Solizslek	Hong.
243	LOWY	Téodor	16/10/27	Cieszyn	Pol.
244	LURIE	Szane	11/4/30	Wilno	"
245	LUSTIG	Laslo	27/10/28	Oradéa	Roum.
246	MAJER	Salomon	26/4/28	Slatuska	Tché.

```
                              - 6 -

            ORPHAN CHILDREN FROM BUCHENWALD NOW IN PARIS

            ENFANTS VENUS D'ALLEMAGNE - CONVOI DU 8 JUIN 1945
                          à ECOUIS (Eure)
                                        Paris List N° II62 A.
```

247	MALICKI	David	I/9/28		Pol.
248	MANDEL	Zaslo	13/II/28	Samaszknzud	Roum.
249	MANDELMANN	Schmul	I/9/27	Lublin	Pol.
250	MARKOWICZ	Szlkim	I6/I/28	Zlomniki	"
25I	Jeno	5/2/28	Somkuta -Mare		Roum/
25I	MARTON	Jeno	5/2/28	Somkuta-Mare	Roum.
252	MECHLOWITS	Mechel	I9/9/29	Slackovce	Tché.
253	MEISNER	Antal	2I/4/28	Sighet	Roum.
254	MENDROWSKI	Jakob	22/I/28	Pow	Pol.
255	MICHALOWICZ	Szymk	2/I2/29	Vichau	"
256	MILS TRAJN	Mendel	5/8/29	Wadezanski	"
257	MILSTEIN	Wolf	28/6/28	Pilica	"
258	MOSKWER	Lolok	I0/I0/29	Kalisz	"
259	MOSKOWICZ	Joseph	I5/8/29	Genisz	Tché.
260	MRCWKA	Beniek	I6/I/32	Debrine	Pol.
26I	MULLER	Laszlo	25/I/28	Oradéa	Roum.
262	NEUWIRTH	Moses	I5/I2/30	Nifcherto	Hong.
263	NICHTHAUSER	Joseph	28/6/28	Bielsko	Pol.
264	NUTOVITS	Zoltan	I7/3/27	Munkecewo	Tché.
265	NUTOVITS	Samuel	I6/6/28	Szdenova	"
266	NUTOVITS	David	I6/3/30	Munkecewo	"
267	OBERLANDER	Mor	24/8/28	Pekas	Hong.
268	OBERZIGGER	Abraham	I4/7/28	Lodz	Pol.
269	ORBACH	Sudek	26/2/24	Czgstoshowie	Pol.
270	ORBACH	Wolf	I/7/29	"	"
27I	ORGEL	Ernest	7/3/27	Simleul	Roum/
272	ORGEL	Bela	5/5/28		"
273	OSTER	Hans	I5/II/28	Koln	Pol.
274	PALUCH	Abraham	I5/2/28	Lodz	"
275	PERELMUTTER	David	8/I/37	"	"
276	PERL	Alexander	8/3/28	Slatwke	Tché.
277	PERL	Herman	I7/4/29	Rozawlia	Roum.
278	PFERFFERMANN	Erwin	28/5/28	Porkumures	"
279	PIEPRZ	Szalaima	20/I2/28	Bedrin	Pol.
280	PODLASKI	John	4/3/9	Lodz	"
28I	POLLAK	Chaim	I0/6/28	Felso	Hongr.
282	POLLAK	Joseph	I8/6/29	Borsa	Roum.
283	POLLAK	Israel	I8/6/29	Borsa	"
284	POMPER	Henryk	27/9/28	Varsovie	Pol.
285	POZNER	Jakob	25/5/30	Veggorka	"
286	PREIZLER	Moritz	7/I/29	Viseul de Sus	Roum.
287	PREIZLER	Monc	I0/5/29	Felso	Hongr.
288	PRZYCCRSKI	Mosrek	I4/8/32	Wtochawek	Pol.
289	REGENBAUM	Ephraim	28/I2/28	Lodz	"
290	RAPAPORT	Major	I2/6/28	Sosnowitz	"
29I	ROSEN	Mieczyst	8/7/28	Lodz	"
292	ROSENBAUM	Hersz	2I/5/28	Bustinazo	Roum.
293	ROSENBAUM	Tibor	I0/II/29	Szalmar	"
294	ROSENBERG	David	20/I/28	Krakow	Pol.
295	ROSENBERG	Herman	3I/7/29	Verchova	"
296	ROSENBERG	Pal	22/II/28	Slajbu	Roum.

- 7 -

ORPHAN CHILDREN FROM BUCHENWALD NOW IN PARIS

ENFANTS VENUS D'ALLEMAGNE – CONVOI DU 8 JUIN 1945
à ECOUIS (Eure)

Paris List N° 1162 A.

297	ROSENBERG	Armin	I/3/28	Zsigot	Roum.
298	ROSENFELD	Zoltan	I3/I/29	Nyiregynsa	Hongr.
299	ROSENKRANC	Ryja	9/I/28	Radzin	"
300	ROSENMAN	Izio	20/5/35	Demblin	Pol.
30I	ROSENTHAL	Samuel	IO/IO/28	Drzelini	"
302	ROSANSKI	Natan	5/II/29	Bedzin	"
303	ROSEN	Morie	9/4/28	Korzewice	"
304	ROZSA	Emevich	29/I/28	Groswareim	Roum.
305	ROTH	Andor	IO/5/28	Peneszlek	Hongr.
306	ROMAN	Penrik	27/9/29	Usworod	Tché.
307	ROTSCHOLD	Salek	II/3/28	Tschenstochau	Pol.
308	RYBSTAJN	Bedek	29/9/30	Strzemieszyce	"
309	RYBSTAJN	Jakob	I5/IO/29	"	"
310	RYPERBAND	Mozes	IO/5/28	"	"
3II	LANDER	Bernat	I5/6/28	Bistrite	Roum.
3I2	SANDOR	Geog.	23/9/28	Croswardeim	"
3I3	SANDOWSKI	Salek	I5/4/28	Piotrkowo	Pol.
3I4	SCHACHTER	Irso	3I/I2/28	Ghimes	Roum.
3I5	CHIFF	Lazar	I7/7/28	Ushorod	Tché.
3I6	SCHIFF	Natan	29/4/29	"	"
3I7	SCHON	Ieno	I/6/IO	Bida	Roum.
3I8	SCHON	Andor	8/6/I3	"	"
3I9	SCHONFELD	Ladislav	23/7/3I	Nybiczldza	Hongr.
320	SWAREBERG	Josek	22/I2/28	Kozienncs	Pol.
32I	SCHWIMMER	Martin	I3/8/28	Knice	Tché.
322	SEGALOWICZ	Isaak	I7/3/30	Lajpeda	Pol.
323	SENDIK	Jakob	IO/4/I7	Lodz	"
324	SENDYK	Abrahm	6/3/28	Lodz	Pol.
325	SENDYK	Samuel	6/8/28	"	"
326	SENDER	Bernard	I5/IO/I4	"	"
327	SILBER	Berek	3/I2/32	Piotrkow	"
328	SILBER	Szyja	29/4/25	"	"
329	SILBERMAN	Moi	I7/I/28	"	Tché.
330	SIMON	Herschz	25/7/28	Rymanow	Pol.
33I	SLOMOVITS	Major	I/9/29	Ruskecole	Tché.
332	SOLNY	Monieck	II/7/29	Trosovice	Pol.
333	SPEIT	Ignac	2/6/28	Oswiecin	"
334	SOLARZ	Monieck	4/4/29	Skamiorz	"
335	STAUBER	Moses	7/2/27		Roum/
336	STEIGER	Josek	I5/8/29	Lodz	Pol.
337	STEIN	Erno	3/7/23	Ujheherto	Hong.
338	STEINBERG	Wolf	IO/IO/28	Ostrowic	Pol.
339	STEINMETZ	Herma	I5/3/29	Marmorussiget	Roum.
340	STENDIG	Lazar	29/6/29	Sarospotok	Hong.
34I	STERN	Mor	27/II/30	Boled	"
342	STERN	Joseph	25/4/28	Wulchowec	Tché.
343	STERN	Jacob	2/5/29	Velki	"
344	STROHL	Sandor	I/I/29	Gyergydhole	Hongr.
345	STERN	Sandor	II/I/28	Satmar	Roum.

- 8 -

ORPHAN CHILDREN FROM BUCHENWALD NOW IN PARIS

ENFANTS VENUS D'ALLEMAGNE - CONVOI DU 8 JUIN 1945
à ECOUIS (Eure)

List N° 1162 A.

346	SYLBIGER	Berek	25/5/28		Pol.
347	SZAFIR	Szymon	25/4/2 9	Wolbrom	"
348	SZCHADMAN	Rubin	10/I/28	Szydlowiec	"
349	SZENFELD	Tibor	30/6/28		Hongr.
350	SZNYGER	Slomon	8/I2/29	Chrzanow	Pol.
35I	SZUCHUS	Lajos	22/I2/29	Gzula	Hongr.
352	SZUFMAN	Berek	2/4/26		Pol.
353	SZWARC	Natan	I0/9/39	Piotrkow	"
354	SAPIRO	Mozès	3/5/32	Kowno	"
355	SZPIGELMAN	Lojb	3/I/28	Strzemiersryce	"
356	SZMELEMAN	Léon	I3/I2/28	Lodz	"
357	SPEKTOR	Abrakaer	I8/I0/29	"	"
358	SZYLKROT	Abram	30/9/3I	Deblin	"
359	TABAK	Martin	I5/5/28	Ujfeherpo	"
360	TARGOWNIK	Szlama	27/I/28	Lodz	"
36I	TOPER	Szulim	25/6/28	Bialobrzegi	"
362	TUSZINSKI	Abraham	27/9/29	Romaszow	"
363	TURAS	Samuel	I5/4/28	Krakovia	"
364	TYSLZER	Jakob	25/4/28	Lodz	"
365	UNGER	Kersoh	I2/9/29	Sosnowiec	"
366	UNIKOWSKI	Israel	9/2/28		"
367	URBACH	Abraham	I/I0/28	Stremieszyce	"
368	VERIEGER	Chaskiel	I6/5/29	Lodz	"
369	VOGEL	Abraham	7/I2/29	Jagora	Tché.
370	VOGELFANG	Henrich	3I/5/28	Maria-Ostro	Pol.
37I	WAJNZTROK	Hugo	9/5/28	Mailsz	"
372	WAGNFELD	Wolf	II/4/30	Lodz	"
373	WAJNGARTEN	Symcha	I4/9/28	Skarjsow	"
374	WAJNSZTATJN	Abram	I0/3/29	Miechow	"
375	WAJSMAN	Romek	2/2/30	Skarsysko	"
376	WAJSSALE	Majloch	4/5/28	Sosnowiec	"
377	WALLER	Beno	22/9/29	Ushorod	Tché.
378	WALTER	Ehoud	3/9/28	Haifa	Roum.
379	WANDERER	Chilwse	25/6/28	Iazcho	Pol.
380	WARSCHAWSLY	Menasse	3/I0/29	Ruwny	"
38I	WARSZAWSKI	Israel	5/5/28	Czestochan	"
382	WARTENBERG	Ludowik	23/9/28	Réglini	Roum.
383	WASSERLAUF	Henick	6/8/27		"
384	WEGH	Michael	24/4/29	Viseul de Sus	
385	WEIL	Imre	I0/6/28	Budapest	Hong.
386	WEINBERGER	Mosès	29/3/28	Nyegyhara	"
387	WEINBERGER	Déssiderius	23/I/28	Nygegherto	"
388	WEINSTEIN	Zelig	I9/5/28	Jaslo	Pol.
389	WEISER	Sigmond	22/I/30	Tasnad	Roum.
390	WEISSTUCH	Chaim	22/7/27	Sosnowiec	Pol.
39I	WEISZ	Martin	4/2/28	Sotmar	Roum/
392	WEISZ	Sandor	II/7/28	Szafmad	Hong.

~ 9 ~

ORPHAN CHILDREN FROM BUCHENWALD NOW IN PARIS

ENFANTS VENUS D'ALLEMAGNE — CONVOI DU 3 JUIN 1945
à ECOUIS (Eure)

List N° 1162 A.

392	WEISZ	Sandor	11/7/28	Szafmad	Hongr.
393	WEISZ	Josef	28/3/28	Munkacevo	Tché.
394	WEISZ	Degto	27/10/28	Csap	"
395	WEISZ	David	13/4/28	Satmar	Roum.
396	WEISZ	Albert	7/1/29	Halmen	"
397	WEISMANN	Ignace	5/1/28	Kosice	Tché.
398	WEIRSEIMANN	Romot	3/9/32	Bendzin	Pol.
399	WENDEL	Josef	23/5/28	Lodz	"
400	WERT	Nebasse	1/5/28	Szczebizezyn	"
401	WIDARSKI	Chaim	11/1/29	Kaskou	"
402	WIBER	Herman	5/5/29	Feldo	Hong.
403	WIEDER	Josef	6/12/28	Segscvoo	Tché.
404	WIEZEN	Ignatz	6/9/29	Rosawla	Roum.
405	WIEZEL	Lazar (ELIE)	4/10/28	Sighet	
406	WILLINGER	Mor	12/12/28	USHOROD	Tché.
407	WIZEL	Majsosz	8/11/29	Lodz	Pol.
408	WROCLAWSKI	Abram	6/12/29	Rawamas	"
409	WRZOWSKI	Dinem	12/3/25	Lodz	"
410	WYGADNY	Ephraim	12/3/28	Lodz	"
411	WZOIER	Salomon	18/1/28	Przemycyce	"
412	ZAKS	Uryn	24/1/28	Klobuck	"
413	ZANDER	Major	14/4/29	Ksioiwielki	"
414	ZEIMANOVICZ	Marton	18/5/29	Ujfgheton	Hong.
415	ZEIT	Herssek	28/3/29	Chmienmik	Pol.
416	ZELIG	Dzso	12/4/28	Des	Roum./
417	ZELIG	Abraham	13/12/28	Bethlen	"
418	ZELIG	Abram	3/5/28		Hong.
419	ZISKIND	Jevoy	10/10/29	Lodz	Pol.
420	ZYSZOVITS	Jeno	5/2/28	Miskolo	Hong.
421	ZOIZEL	Savi	28/3/28		Tché.
422	ZOZILSKI	Marek	20/1/29		Pol.
423	ZYLBERBERG	Sara	4/12/25	Radom	"
424	ZYLBERBERG	Israel	6/10/28	"	"
425	ZYLBERFEND	Szema	7/5/28	Chrzalow	"
426	ZYLBERSTAJN	Chaim	23/12/28	Varsovie	"

✠ ELIE WIBSEL

SELECTED READINGS

- Hochberg-Mariańska, Maria, and Noe Grüss. *The Children Accuse*. London, Portland, OR: Valentine Mitchell, 1996.

  This remarkable book was originally published in Polish by the Jewish Historical Commission in Cracow, 1946. Its author interviewed surviving children already in 1945 immediately after the war. There is no question of suppressed or faded memory. The revelations of horrors are fresh.

  Hochberg-Mariańska talked with children who survived in ghettos and camps and in hiding. The first children she met were from Auschwitz-Birkenau, boys and girls from the age of four. She writes, "As I sat among them, listening to their stories, all my own experiences in the resistance, all the years of working and fighting seemed insignificant and feeble, something unworthy of being mentioned in comparison with their terror and their quiet children's suffering and heroism. For Jewish children not only died, stayed in hiding or ran away from their executioners; they fought for their lives on all fronts in this uneven battle."

- Krell, Robert and Marc I. Sherman. *Medical and Psychological Effects of Concentration Camps on Holocaust Survivors*. Volume 4, in Genocide: A Critical Bibliographic Review (ed. I.W. Charny), New Brunswick (USA), London (UK): Transaction, 1997.

  This book comprises two essays, "Psychiatry and the Holocaust" and "Survivors and Their Families: Psychiatric Consequences of the Holocaust" as well as 2,461 references to the literature 1945-1995, and an annotated bibliography of 49 books. Ten books reviewed pertain to children specifically and five to children of survivors.

- Lau-Lavie, Naphtali. *Balaam's Prophecy: Eyewitness to History 1939-1989*. London: Cornwall Books. 1997.

  After concentrating his considerable energies in defense of the State of Israel, as a soldier, writer, spokesman for the Ministry of Defence and Israeli Consul-General in New York, Naphtali Lavie sums up his life's work. This powerful memoir includes his years of suffering in Nazi death camps as well as his years involved in the political process ensuring the survival of the Jewish state.

- Rouveyre, Miriam. *Enfants de Buchenwald* Éditions Juillard, 20, rue des Grands-Augustins, 75006 Paris (French), 1995.

     In Buchenwald, there existed an internal resistance organization which assumed responsibility to protect children. The youngest of them was four-year-old Juschu.

     The author traces the history of the establishment of Buchenwald and of the resistance formed primarily of long-time non-Jewish inmates, the anti-Fascist political prisoners. Block 8 was organized to house the majority of children, followed later by Block 66.

     Eyewitness accounts of these developments were offered by Henri Dymant, Jacques Zilbermine, Aron Bulwa, Élie Buzyn, David Perlmutter, Izio Schaechter and Willy Fogel.

     The last days of Buchenwald are recounted as well as the final murderous deportations of thousands of Jews to Flossenberg and Dachau. Few survived these journeys.

     On June 8, 1945, 426 children and adolescents arrived at Écouis, 210 Polish Jews, 118 Rumanians, 49 Czechs, 43 Hungarians, 4 Lithuanians and 2 German Jews.

- Śliwowska, Wiktoria (Ed.). *The Last Eyewitnesses, Children of the Holocaust Speak*. Evanston, Illinois: Northwestern University Press, 1998.

     This book contains dozens of eyewitness accounts, many dating back to 1945, when they were first recorded in Poland. Others were submitted later, primarily in 1991-1992, when Polish-Jewish child survivors formed an association.

     Young concentration camps survivors sent in their accounts from Warsaw, Wroclaw, Lodz, Rome, and several were written in 1945 in Zatrzebie.

- Wiesel, Elie. *Night*. New York, Toronto, London, Sydney: Bantam Books, 1982.

     First published in French in 1958, this slim volume of 109 pages can be read in a few hours, then contemplated for a lifetime. Its power remains undiminished over time. "Night" is required reading for anyone learning about the Shoah.

- Wiesel, Elie. *Memoirs: All Rivers Run to the Sea*. New York: Alfred A. Knopf, 1995, and *The Sea Is Never Full. Memoirs 1969*. New York: Alfred A. Knopf, 1999.

     Two volumes of reminiscences filled with tragedy and humour, lessons and insights, challenges and accusations. Elie Wiesel reveals, with candour and restraint, his struggle to be faithful to memory and translate that memory into action in service of the oppressed. He sides with the victim, those so frequently without representation or voice. He accuses the bystander and his or her silence, since silence almost always assists the oppressor.

Elie Wiesel's life spans many of the crucial events of the century. His reflections on Taverny shed further light on the importance of that period of transition from Buchenwald to post-war life.

Articles

1. Hemmendinger, Judith (1994) The children of Buchenwald: After liberation and now. *Echoes of the Holocaust* 3, 40-51. [Bulletin of the Jerusalem Center for Research into the Late Effects of the Holocaust. Talbieh Mental Health Center, Jerusalem, Israel].
2. Jouhy, E. (1946) Le problème pedagogique des jeunes de Buchenwald. Geneva: Union OSE, pp.59-66.
3. Kestenberg, Judith S. (1992) Children under the Nazi yoke. *British Journal of Psychotherapy*, 8(4), 374-390.
4. Krell, Robert (1985) Therapeutic value of documenting child survivors. *Journal of the American Academy of Child Psychiatry* 24(4), 397-400.
5. Krell, Robert (1993) Child survivors of the Holocaust: Strategies of adaptation. *Canadian Journal of Psychiatry*, 38(6), 384-389.
6. Minkowski, E. (1946) Les Enfants de Buchenwald. Geneva: Union OSE, pp.27-59.
7. Moskovitz, Sarah, and Krell, Robert (1990) Child survivors of the Holocaust: Psychological adaptations to survival. *Israel Journal of Psychiatry and Related Sciences*, 27(2), 81-91.